To ,

Animal Talking Tales

Jackie Weaver

With best wishes and thank you for your support over the years.

Jackie x.

Local Legend Publishing UK

Other books by Jackie Weaver: Animal Insight

www.animaltalking.co.uk

A Record of this Publication is available
from the British Library

ISBN 978-1-907203-21-3

Local Legend Publishing 2010
Park Issa
St Martin's Road
Gobowen, Shropshire
SY11 3NP, UK
www.local-legend.co.uk

Cover Design by Titanium Design Ltd
www.titaniumdesign.co.uk

For Bob, Sally and my friends
for their constant love, help and support,
and for being with me to share the precious
moments that this wonderful gift of
Animal Communication brings.

I would like to thank Jackie Fennell, my great and talented friend for all the beautiful artwork she has done for this book. Also to Jan Meakin for her friendship, generosity of time and for being there with her wise words. Also to Jacky Newcomb and Jenny Smedley for their support and enthusiasm in helping me spread the word about animal communication and the wonders it can achieve.

"If you have opened this book and are reading this, then you are either a believer or curious and therefore open to persuasion. Trust me, Jackie talks to animals. She is not alone – I know of other people who are able to communicate with our furry companions in this way, but she has the added gift of a sense of humour. These are marvellous, heart warming, funny, touching stories that give us a breathtaking insight into our animals and the way they live their lives and relate to us.

I hope you enjoy them as much as I did."

Jenny Seagrove

Table of Contents

Foreword - Introduction

Since my first book, *Animal Insight,* I have been overwhelmed by people's responses and absolutely delighted how I have managed to help get the word out there. More and more people are coming round to the idea that animals can and do talk which is where my work as an Animal Communicator comes in.

I am now four years past the cancer which the doctors thought would have claimed my life as it had spread throughout my body invading everywhere it could. Having survived the treatment, which to be honest seems like a distant blurred memory, I am actually now in very good health and cramming as much into every day that I can. If there is one thing a near-death-experience teaches you it is that 'life is precious', and, if you are lucky like me, an extra gift becomes apparent with it. My gift is being able to hear on the same 'wavelength' as animals so they can relay their words and thoughts to me, to pass on to their owners. Although I do not make promises to anyone, my work has been proven again and again, and I have been so fortunate to be in a position to change things in animals' lives.

This book is another selection of real cases about animals that I have talked with, and listened to. I promise you, they can talk and they understand what we say to them, and so much more. They are personalities like ourselves but the difference is, apart from the obvious, that they are far more accepting of their lot than we are. They don't crave the latest designer goods or are envious of others' status in life; they just want and need love, understanding, and to be respected as another living being. Basically, animals are very honest and that is how the animal kingdom exists. Don't get me wrong, they are not all 'little angels' out there, quite the opposite in fact, and I take great joy in listening to what they most certainly do on purpose but with that look of complete innocence, so well practised.

I work with complete honesty and think my 'job' is one of the top ten in the world. Most people can only converse with other humans, but I get to chat not only to people but with many different species of animals too. I do have to deal with sadness but I spend so much of my time laughing with the animals and their owners that I would truly say to anyone, even when your chips are down, don't give up, you never know what is round the corner. If a miracle can happen for me, then why not for you? What is for you will not go past you.

I have found by experience that by the time people had read half way through my previous book, they agreed that there was no way it could be all just a figment of my imagination and this has changed the way they see animals forever. I hope this book does the same for you and gives you hope and joy reading it. I know that all people have varying views and some people think that this life on Earth finishes here, and that is that. Everyone is entitled to their own beliefs and I respect that, but animals, again and again, have gone out of their way to show me differently, and that has been such a great comfort to their owners left behind. You will also be amazed how animals seem to come into people's lives for a reason and if you think of it yourself, how many times did you have no intention of getting another one, but somehow you did?!

There are so many more wonderful things in this world that we are not aware of, my work is the tip of the iceberg. To quote the words of a very wise man, "Listen and you shall see!" Or in this case, 'Read and you shall see!' Don't get me wrong, as life can be hard, and seemingly very unfair at times, but whatever happens, there is always a lesson in there. Believe it or not, for every negative there is a positive, though sometimes you have to search very hard for it, but usually you will find, 'Every cloud does have a silver lining'.

All the stories are absolutely genuine. I have changed some identities for obvious reasons, but it has also been my great pleasure to have been asked to include proper names in many stories as the owners are happy to share their personal experiences with readers.

I hope to make you laugh, and may even bring a tear to your eye. I have also included a few of my own little life's exploits in here too and hope that you truly enjoy sharing a little piece of my wonderful world with me.

As in my previous book too, I have included the Animal Titbits so we can have some more funny, sweet and 'saying it as it is' comments straight from the animals' mouths.

Smelly-vision

As I have said, my life is full of laughter and fun and I truly believe that it does help the world go round. When I start a call, I always ask if they have done communication before and rarely the answer is 'yes'. For a few, they have experienced it where it is just sent back in writing to them, basically answering questions that have been asked or what information the animal has volunteered. The reason I do it 'live' on the phone is that if you are having a conversation with someone often it leads in a different direction to that which you would have first thought. I explain to people to look on this like a conversation with a child, so if you can bear in mind the saying 'never work with children or animals' you can imagine what often happens when I talk to animals that love being childish!!

When 'reading' I get passed over sound, vision and physical pain, which I acknowledge straight away, so it then stops. This is my way of confirming it is definitely not mine, it belongs to the animal I am talking to. I also feel emotions and get various smells too.

When I am talking, sometimes my voice will rise with tension that I am getting passed from the animal and even sometimes with a brusque attitude, which I quickly point out is not me personally being 'sharp' but that is how the animal is talking. This obviously tends to be with animals that are having problems in some way or ones that have 'attitude'. On the other hand, I have been known to burst out laughing when, for example, I find out an animal loves being tickled on his tummy and they have literally passed it over to me to experience. Animals do not ever divulge improper personal information, so people never have to worry about that, and I know that my guides would never pass it on to me anyway. Animals do have a great sense of humour and a lovely one that springs to mind was when my friend, Rhiannon, her sister and parents came to visit me. I landed up chatting to their dog, as you do! She was a lovely dog and took great delight in showing her prowess as a comedian. She gave me phrases like, 'I just don't think my mouth is wide enough!' which caused us to laugh as, apparently, as soon as she gets to the woods she chooses the largest stick she can find and tries to run between the trees with it and invariably comes unstuck, well, 'stuck' to be precise! Her owners now just wait for her to do it and it gets the same jovial reception every time. She had learnt that this made them laugh so she often did it, but without causing any actual physical harm to herself. Whilst we were laughing about the fact that animals really do things on purpose, Rhiannon's father suddenly asked if I would ask his dog what she thought of him. And as soon as those words left his lips she announced to me, without a pause but with a certain phoney air of innocence, "I am under the impression that he doesn't change his socks every day!!" Well, if you can imagine, I just fell about laughing and asked him if he really wanted to hear what she had said? Egged on by his wife, Rhiannon and her sister, I repeated it to him.

He smiled and scrunched his eyes a bit and said, "Err, I have been known to forget to change them!!" And, even more bizarrely, in the midst of this communication, we had a discussion about who really do change their socks every day, so Lord knows what this dog thought she had started!

One day I drove onto a yard I had been to several times before with my husband, Bob, as he has been Carolyn's horse dentist for years. During his last dental visit with me going along for the ride, somehow I ended up having an impromptu chat with one of her horses. On this visit, though, it was only me as she had asked me to come and chat to all four of them. They were great fun and very informative, although the one horse kept butting in all the time, as sometimes happens with a strong personality. He, in fact, was the one that I had spoken to previously, and on that occasion when I asked if he had any helpful advice for Carolyn, he wanted to let her know that he thought there was some wiring which was unsafe. I pushed for a more in-depth explanation and he showed me a thick wire that seemed to be attached to what looked like a wooden plank! I had no idea what it was he was talking about, as neither did Carolyn. I told her not to worry, however, if there was a problem maybe look for wiring attached somewhere, like the picture he was describing. She nodded and said if a problem occurred she would pass his information on to her landlord! I had totally forgotten about this nugget of information until it was brought to my attention on another occasion when, during a chat with one of the horses, the yard owner appeared and, without hesitation, Carolyn introduced me by saying, "This is Jackie who saved your house being burnt down!!"

He looked at me, nodded and said, "Thank you very much!" and walked on. I laughed and then listened as she regaled the story about how the power had kept on shorting out and then an electrician had found an exposed live wire touching a smouldering wooden slat behind an electric fuse board. Once again a horse had informed us of something that was absolutely true, and somehow he just knew! As I explained, animals are 'open' and do know things (there are more examples throughout this book), so I tend to listen and pass on things, but carefully put it so as not to cause alarm.

I finished the chats when she suddenly remembered a question that she wanted to ask of the noisy horse that kept interrupting. Could I please ask him what he thought of Bob?! Now bearing in mind some horses do not like having their teeth done but most, on the whole, are pretty good about it, I thought this could be interesting. I also knew through booking Bob's calls that she had at least one sedated on the yard but I did not know if it was him. I simply put it to him, "What do you think of Bob, your dentist?"

And his reply, "Oh he's nice, but he smells like a girl!!" Well we just fell about laughing and if you are wondering why, this is the reason; Bob puts lavender on the front of his tunic so the horses can inhale the aroma while he is working on their teeth. He thinks it does help to keep some calm and even if it doesn't, it does make him smell a bit more pleasant after spending hours working in horses' stables.

I had absolute joy talking to a miniature horse in California who was just the bees knees (any idea of how and why that saying was invented?! Answers on a postcard please!) to talk to. He was really just like a big dog and very full of himself. He would pick things up and carry them about and generally make everyone laugh, including me! One question that did make me think was when she said, "Can you ask him about the wildlife that he encounters?"

Now bearing in mind I am not good with geography and even worse about what animal inhabits what part of the world, I had one of those momentary panics thinking, what if it is a puma or something like that? My fears were quickly dismissed when I saw something dark, bigger than a rat though, and just as I went into its description I was given the most awful nasty niff to go with it, and as I uttered about the smell, she so casually said, "Oh, that'll be the skunk then!!" This pony didn't complain but said that he wished it would take a wider berth!

About a year ago, I came up with the format for a show that I hope will be very entertaining and a completely new 'take' on animal communication. My aim in life is that the more that people experience it, they will then believe in it and then animals will benefit from it. So with my printed-up format, a couple of very good friends, Sal and Jackie (known as Jacks, also the artist for this book) said they would help me practise and see how it flowed. So, sitting in Jack's kitchen with a video camera perched on the counter we set about practising the show with Sal being the 'compère'. The 'contestant's' pets, Eddie and Alfie, consisted of one Labrador and one Labrador cross Spaniel, which sounds fine, but they were only ten months old!! So Sal had her script to hand, we set the camera rolling and I started doing my animal chatting to practise this idea of mine. Well, all was going smoothly and what they were saying was correct, but Alfie and Eddie decided it would be good to have a bit of rough and tumble to liven up the proceedings and started getting rather boisterous, to say the least! As much as Jacks tried to concentrate she couldn't and asked, "Are you sure they are listening to us?!"

"Oh, yes", I replied, "it's to their subconscious, so don't worry!" As much as we tried, it really was one of those 'animals and children' cases and we were struggling not to laugh but we were failing and, to make matters worse, an unfortunate aroma made itself apparent, and no, this was not telepathic, this was real and was hanging in the air like a very dark and obvious cloud! I was nearest the culprit and couldn't speak for laughing but as Sal was urging me to 'get on with it' and bearing in mind this was being filmed I discreetly said, behind my hand, "One of the dogs has 'dropped' one", and, just at that point, Sal and Jacks got their own waft too!

Then, unbelievably, Sal announces, as loud as you like to the video camera, as if it was an audience, "Oh, we do apologise, Mrs Weaver has completely lost it as one of the dogs has just *blown orf*!" and said with the utmost essence of someone speaking the proper Queen's English. Well, that was it, all finesse had been dispersed with and we were like three school kids who couldn't string a sensible sentence together between us! As much as we tried, we just kept laughing, so abandoned that run through. Fortunately, as it had been recorded, I was able to cut the clip out of the bedlam and send it to various friends showing just how crazy and funny life can be. We have practised since and one day I will use the format to spread the word, and thank goodness I can work from a distance!!

Jackie Weaver

Nearly Down the Road

When the first words you hear on a phone call are, "Help, my horse may need to be put down," this would instil an immediate angst into anyone, and I am no exception.

About six months previously, I had been doing some 'chatting for charity' in a local 'horsey' country store. This lovely lady, Avril, came to my table and asked if I could chat to her horse for her. She sat down and introduced herself and her niece, and gave me a picture of a dark bay thoroughbred gelding, Haut Cercy (Cercy for short), who was then twelve and had finished his racing days, as had Avril. There are racing yards everywhere, some with hundreds of horses and, although this was a big yard, every horse was known individually and this one especially. Cercy had been looked after by Avril who was his groom for all of his time with the yard. He was a hugely talented horse and won many steeplechases and just as he was to run the race of his life - The Grand National - he broke down as his tendons ruptured on not one front leg but both. Although obviously very disappointed that 'her' horse wasn't going to run, she adored him and his health and well-being was of paramount importance to her. In many yards, sadly, a high percentage of horses in this physical condition are thought to have no purpose left for the trainers and often their lives come to an untimely end. Not for this horse though; He was nursed back to health by Avril and his owner, and amazingly Avril was told that when she left she could take him with her, which is exactly what she did!

Bear in mind that this chat was taking part in the middle of a large shop with many people milling about, but Avril didn't care that tears were falling down her cheeks as Cercy was thanking her and telling her that he knew how much she had loved and cared for him and that they were destined to be together. It wasn't the longest of chats, as with the charity ones, I try to get through as many as I can in the time I am there. Just as we finished, her niece's mobile rang and I was staggered to hear it was the same ringtone as mine. Now, that might not sound unusual but I had made my own ringtone by recording an excerpt of music by Guns and Roses (I know, don't laugh!) and here was a young girl playing the same tune that she had properly downloaded! Come on, what were the chances of that phone ringing at that time...?! Anyway, it certainly helped dry up Avril's tears as I searched under my table, found my mobile and proceeded to play the evidence!

Many months later, Avril booked Bob to come and look at her horse's teeth and I recognised her name and said that I would try to come along as well. We had got the directions and found it easily and as we drove in the yard, she simply leant through my passenger window, kissed me on the cheek and said, "I love this woman, she is amazing!" I have never forgotten that, and it makes me smile every time I see her.

Back to the phone call… Hanna, Avril's friend, was having major problems with her horse, another ex-racehorse called Gillimar (Gilly for short). Having heard the first lines of this distressed mobile call, I quickly ascertained that the horse was not critically ill at that point so suggested she follow my usual booking procedure,(animal's photo, age and owner's details etc.) I would treat her as a priority. Within hours I was talking to this horse and had no idea what I would be facing, whether this was physical or mental, or both.

As soon as I started talking to Gilly he gave me the feeling of being 'all over the place' – 'stressy', uneasy and not really knowing what he should say or do. He made me physically so uncomfortable; I felt like I wanted to curve my back to one side! He was an ex-racehorse and was just totally 'messed up' as physically he was so sore and, as much as Hanna loved him and tried with him, he was being classed as dangerous. I now realised that it was due to his behaviour that the suggestion had been made to have him put down, so I said to Hanna that most horses feeling as uncomfortable as this would behave the same way, so at least we knew there was a cause. Although I had to keep stopping Hanna telling me too much, I said that I thought she was right - underneath he was the loving horse she had thought he was, but not to get her hopes up too high, but if this was all as he was giving it to me, we might be in with a chance.

I asked him for an example of what he was doing when ridden and Gilly showed him getting increasingly stressed and leaping about, explained cleverly by the description, "I am like a sewing machine going wrong, the more up and down I go, the more material gets snagged underneath." Hanna said that was actually a very good depiction. This had happened on several occasions I asked him to try to show me what was bringing it on. He showed me the road, then going up a very steep hill with another horse in front, and it was as if he was getting left behind and was being urged on. This was exactly as it had happened but, unfortunately, the more she pushed, the more discomfort he had and now could no longer tolerate any of it, so, in his best way, reacted to get her to stop. This caused her to fall off and land on the road, which, as any horse rider knows, is a totally unforgiving landing surface. This hadn't been the first time it had happened either and Hanna said she knew it hadn't been a traffic problem as he didn't worry about cars and lorries passing. She was still upset but asked what she could do to 'fix' him. I suggested that I should scan over his body and see what was wrong but before doing quickly reeled off my 'I do not diagnose, I will just tell you what he gives me' spiel.

Well, where was I to start? He threw everything at me as quickly as he could. He had horrible sharp teeth, which he was forced to endure the pain of even more as someone had suggested that Hanna should use a crank noseband to keep his mouth shut. Being a horse rider and dentist's wife, I am aware that a small percentage of horses will insist on opening their mouth whilst ridden, but a huge percentage are doing it to get away from the discomfort inside. There are many types of tooth problem but the main one is sharp edges. What exactly do we mean by 'sharp' relevant to horses teeth? Maybe an odd bit here and there that is not terribly smooth? Well I can assure you, having seen many lacerated mouths and the cuts and slices on my husband's hands, horses' teeth can be like razors and sit just in the right place to cut the inside of their lovely soft cheeks. If we get a 'sharp bit' ourselves it can be so annoying, so try imagining having four full rows of them. With his head tilted right, his neck 'out', withers wrong and his right pelvis dropped, I could now see where the curve came from, so I said to her, "It is like he is bent like a banana!" On top of that, he had a really 'stressy' stomach which I think was being exacerbated by all that was going on. Plus, one saddle she had been using was a poor fit but she had another now and was going to get a saddler to check it fitted him properly.

Please do not get me wrong, Hanna was not purposely being mean, but all the various things would have only been picked up by those with an experienced eye, and she was just doing her best. I asked him what else he thought would help, and he said he would like probiotics and some sort of herb/flower (?) to help with his stress. Hanna volunteered that she knew just the person to help with that.

If I talk to horses that live in my area and teeth problems become apparent, I find it difficult as I do not want to appear as if I am looking for work for Bob but have to be honest to the horse and owner. On this occasion, it suddenly sprang to my mind that Bob was booked out very near to where she lived, so I asked her if she wanted him to pop in and check him. Bearing in mind that Hanna had not had a dentist to Gilly, and Bob did her friend Avril's horses, she said that would be brilliant. She asked where he would be coming from and when I told her the name, she laughed and said that it was her who had recommended they get Bob in the first place and that is where she kept Gilly! She had not thought of getting Gilly's teeth done as she was under the impression that that had been done just prior to her getting him. I asked her to let me know how she got on, and she said that she would get everything else done after Bob had seen to his 'front end'. (A case point here: if you are having recurrent back problems, always make sure the teeth are in good order. If you think of this logically, when we have teeth problems we will often tilt our head or eat on one side and, in turn, we can get an aching neck and that is without contending with a bit in our mouths either! So, for a horse, if it's not moving mechanically right at the front end, it will then start to cause problems further back).

Gilly got his teeth done and I have to admit I was rather worried as I had not heard anything for a while, but when I did, it totally validated this work I do. Here is part of the email Hanna sent to me:

'Hi Jackie,

Sorry it's been a long time but I have been very busy with Gilly! All good!!!!!!!!

Since you helped me find out about the problems Gilly was suffering from, he has turned into the most lovable, caring, and friendly horse I have ever had the pleasure of knowing!

During his session he told you about his teeth, his head, withers, back, pelvis, saddle and stomach, and the wanting of a flower. Well, first of all, Bob came and did his teeth and he said there were problems and sorted them out! Then I got in touch with Sarah Smith, the chiropractor, to come and give him a once-over. She found that his poll was out, as were his withers and his back and his pelvis had dropped on one side! He was then given two weeks off to chill! Oh yes, I started feeding him natural yoghurt for his probiotics to help his stomach too! Then came the turn of Amanda, the saddler, and the freakiest thing happened! When she was standing behind Gilly looking down his back, she turned and looked at me and said, "Your horse is shaped like a banana!" If you recall, Gilly said to you he felt like a banana! The new saddle I bought for him, just before we spoke, did fit him but the old one, definitely did NOT! Then whilst telling my friend about Gilly she told me her mum was studying flower oil treatment in animals and asked if she could use Gilly as a case study! Of course, I said yes! She was with us for two hours. The second oil she offered him was Linden Blossom which he could not get enough of and I still offer it to him now and he still takes it, but not as much. Linden blossom is used for trauma and abuse which I felt deep down inside he was suffering from. Now things are amazing! We can go through open fields, ride in company and, touch wood, he has not had a 'wonky' moment since! He gallops round the field bucking which I have never seen him do before! He gallops up to me in the field shouting at me. I love him so much and I know he does me too! So thank you so much for helping us both! I have told all of my friends and some have been in touch with you and they, like me, are just so very grateful to you!

Hanna and Gilly'

A Quick Return

In life, timing is everything and I truly believe that we are often put in the 'right place at the right time'. I keep this principle in my head when I am at a venue and things don't go quite according to plan.

This was one such occasion when a friend had suggested it would be a great idea for me to attend one that was a regular event at a hotel in a nearby town. I phoned the fair organiser and he said by chance there was a spare table as a regular clairvoyant was unavailable so I could come and see how it goes! It started at ten o'clock. By twelve I had done no work whatsoever and I was that bored I was actually helping hand out show tickets and leaflets on behalf of the organiser! Lunchtime came and one of the clairvoyants asked me to talk to her cat that was actually in France with a friend of hers; this clairvoyant would tour round Britain and then return home for a well-deserved holiday. She bought me a posh prawn sandwich and I found out her cat was coping well with her absences and much preferred her freedom over there than to her previous house in the UK.

Two o'clock was looming and I was really wishing I could leave when a middle-aged lady approached me for a reading, but she thought I was 'doing people' and when I explained about animals she said, "Ah, you are just the person I need!" She sat down, accompanied by her friend, and gave me the description of her little dog, Tinker (Tinks for short), who was a black Jack Russell aged about ten months. Well, as much as I tried to talk to this little girl she was snubbing me big style and, in the end turned her back on me!!

I was beginning to think my day was going to be completely sunk and just simply said, "This might sound bizarre but she has just turned her back on me and is certainly giving me a bit of attitude!"

"That sounds just like her!" replied her owner Diane. I breathed a sigh of relief as I now knew I had connected with Tinks but felt I really had my work cut out.

I tried the niceties like, 'What do you like that makes you happy?' But she rebuffed me again and again, so in the end I suggested that Diane ask me a relevant question. She asked if I could ask her about the weeing. I asked Tinks if she would like to tell me what Diane was talking about and with that she succinctly replied, "They really didn't want me, so I do as I please, thanks!"

"What do you mean?" I queried.

"You ask her," Tinks suggested, with obvious irritation, I might add, so I carefully put this to Diane. As I said it I saw the tears well up in Diane's eyes, and her friend gave her a hug, so I knew that I had hit a raw nerve. I told her not to worry, whatever it was we will try and undo what seems to be wrong and encouraged her to share it with me. Diane told me that she and her husband had always had Greyhounds throughout their married life. After their last faithful friend had died the family presented them with this little six-week-old pup, namely this little dog, Tinks, which they thought would be far more suitable. Diane felt guilty as she recalled that she admitted she told the family, in no uncertain terms, that she did not want this dog, and a terrier at that. Diane did not dislike this innocent pup personally, but a Jack Russell was about as far away from a Greyhound as a Shetland pony would be from a Thoroughbred horse.

Diane quickly said, "But I have grown to love her, only she wees everywhere and anywhere, she even goes to my daughter's house, runs upstairs and wees there."

I now understood why this little dog was coming over as very agitated: she had felt unwanted and basically taken umbrage, and was not forgiving them whatsoever – well, until this point, where I was going to attempt to try and undo the emotional damage. Tinks decided to talk to me and did tell me that they gave her toys and balls and that she wanted for nothing, BUT hated being shut in the kitchen! Ah, I thought we have a bargaining tool here. So I confirmed that she was shut in there as she could not be trusted not to wee wherever she pleased. We discussed the toilet routine and Diane said that she even went home at lunchtime to let her out and, as much as she tried to get her to go, she simply wouldn't. But, as soon as she went back inside she would pee and look defiantly as if to say, "Yeah, and??"

I did manage to (well, hoped I had) get Tinks to realise that what she hated was occurring due to her own actions and should she comply and do a wee outside like all other dogs do, she would then have the run of the house...well, two actually! She thought hard and said that would be better and mentioned that there was a picture up of her, as well as the Greyhounds, so she knew that they did love her really. I asked Tinks what Diane could say (this I call a 'bonding key' which are words to hopefully prick the subconscious to remember the conversation) to encourage her, and she offered, "If you need to go, go now, and you won't be shut in the kitchen anymore!" Diane was polite enough to say she would try it but, to be honest, neither of us held out much hope.

With Tink's chat over, Diane's friend, Pat, gave me a photo of her little Yorkie, Lucky, who was the sweetest and most adorable little boy. He started chatting straightaway away which made a very welcome change. He was typically the apple of her eye and it was such a joy to be able to tell Pat lovely personal things from her dog. Lucky was one of those very small ones that look like a fluffy toy, and was very much a lap dog for Pat and was her constant companion through those long winter evenings. The one worry Pat had was that Lucky was making a snuffling sound and the vets had decided the best option was to anaesthetise him to look up inside his nose. They suspected he may have polyps, or something similar, and would try to remove them if possible. I asked Lucky if he understood this and he informed me that he didn't think the noise was coming from his nose, but lower down in his chest. I mentioned this to Pat and she shook her head and said she wouldn't know. I said that I could ask Lucky what he thought might help his condition and he said something that sounded like, "Lungwort!" Well, that stumped me; I had no idea what Lungwort was, but asked Pat if she happened to know.

"Oh yes, we have some in the garden and, come to think of it, he keeps putting his nose in it!"

"I think I could use it to make him a herbal tea." Pat suggested. I made it very clear that I would not personally advocate anybody to make, do, or give an animal any remedy without checking with their vet first but it turned out though, that Pat was into herbal remedies and assured me she would be very careful. I finished the chat and wished them both well.

It still amazes me when an animal will mention to me a fairly obscure treatment, and I look them up on the internet afterwards, as I did this one, and sure enough, it is widely used for respiratory problems, hence the name *Lung*wort. People have often said to me, 'But we cannot diagnose ourselves, so how can animals?' Well, we say we can't, but actually that is maybe because we are just following what we have been taught. For example, Native Americans are taught their own method of self-healing which is far removed from Western medicine and they can diagnose/heal themselves. My personal theory is that animals ask their guides (why should guides be exclusive to us?!) and they are given the answers, the same way as my guide helps me.

The clock had ticked onwards and it was nearly five o'clock and, as I was packing up, people were filing in for the mediumship demonstrations that would close the event. In front of me appeared a smiling Diane, and, with a sense of shock said, "I nipped back home to take Tinks out for her usual walk around the block and used the words she said and… She did a wee!! I was so staggered; I just had to come back here to tell you. To be honest, I didn't really think it would work but it did, and I will keep you informed, thank you." I smiled and thanked her for her kindness in coming back to let me know and felt that at least I had achieved what I was obviously there to do.

To be honest, I had forgotten all about that day when an email popped in from Diane. She said that Tinks now had the freedom of the house but could she pay for another reading as her husband had not really believed her so she would write everything down this time! Tinks was truly happier and had forgotten all about her bad start and, during that conversation I also found out that Pat's dog, Lucky, had lapped up his herbal tea and did not have an operation after all!

Diane finished the call, leaving her to go and repeat everything to her husband and see if it was still all a 'coincidence'! I did laugh when the next day another email arrived from her. Having gone over it with her husband, they had come up with an important question: "Ages ago we lost a ping pong ball, at first we thought Tinks might have eaten it but we realised, on reflection, she would have choked rather than swallowed it, but we have searched high and low, and just wondered..."

No, I didn't go into the missing ball query but I emailed back thanking them for giving me a good giggle about such an 'important' question especially from someone who previously was a non-believer!

On the Spot

On a warm summer's day, Bob and I decided to take a detour and call in on someone we had not seen for a while as we had moved and they were now a fair distance away from us. They live at this very old-fashioned farm, complete with the terriers and a couple of hound puppies being 'walked'. Well, if you have had any personal experience of hound puppies, the expression 'walked' is far removed from what they tend to do! They are big, boisterous and friendly but believe you me, they are absolute monkeys!! On one occasion Bob was working on some horses' teeth, he turned round and they had quietly, but deliberately, removed one of the rasps from his bucket and were merrily playing tug of war with it!

Sarah and Dave were both at home and invited us in to their kitchen for a cuppa, where we were greeted by a selection of Norfolk and Jack Russell terriers. It really is a case of 'one off, one on', hence when leaving there you look like you have grown a 'dog hair sporran!"

While we were catching up on all the latest happenings Sarah happened to mention they were having a big problem with one of their stallions. I say 'big' problem, but it was actually with their smallest stallion, a Welsh Mountain pony called Merlin. He was about nine years old, a registered Section A, which to be correct for the breed should not be over 11.3 hands and have quite a bit of substance about them, comparative to the Section B, which sometimes look like mini racehorses. The Welsh farmers used to use them on the hills for checking and rounding up their sheep, so they are strong and versatile little ponies. If you don't think I get nervous, on some occasions I still do, and as much as I glossed over the conversation, my dear husband was saying, "Jackie will ask him for you, won't you Jackie?" I discreetly shot that 'look': 'Please be quiet', but agreed that after our coffee we could go and see him.

You might not understand my reluctance, but let me explain to you why. Firstly, I knew that a vet had looked over this pony from top to bottom, and secondly, Dave, whom we have known for several years, is extremely clever at the work he does diagnosing and treating horses. He works in a holistic way and often identifies things that the vets would have struggled to find. If anyone has studied Shiatsu or

Acupuncture you will be aware that there are 'points' all over bodies that relate to the inner and outer parts of the body. It is quite like understanding a huge electrical circuit and knowing where every source of power is going and when there is resistance, why and what it is related to. So my doubting thought process was, 'That if *he* can't pinpoint it, then how serious is this and will Merlin be able to get it over to me?' My doubting process was also being compounded with the fact that I was under the impression that Sarah was definitely a sceptic. Anyway, with coffee drunk and the world put to rights we headed up the yard to the stables where Merlin was kept.

Dave stayed at the barn entrance whilst Sarah and I made our way up to the far end where Merlin was stabled. On the way, Sarah proceeded to pick up a headcollar but I told her that we didn't need one as I didn't need him out; I would talk to him from outside the stable. I positioned myself with my back to him but facing Sarah, who immediately noticed and asked, "Don't you want to look at him?"

"No," I replied, "if I look at him it might give me some guidance as to what is going on, so I would rather not be influenced in any direction." This is why when I work from a photograph 'at a distance' then people's scepticism diminishes very quickly as I have not got any physical evidence of symptoms or behaviour, yet I can relay it to them.

I started the chat with Merlin and asked him to tell me something about himself. He declared he was very gentle and not worth the money he used to be! Sarah told me I was right on both counts so I proceeded further. With that, he made me 'grab' my stomach, and I relayed the spasmodic feeling I was getting inside. Sarah acknowledged it and asked if there was anything else, so I was thinking that maybe that wasn't relevant to what they were looking for. He then gave me an obvious dull ache in the top area of my right leg, with the explanation that he had fallen off the side of a mare he was trying to mount! Sarah said she was unaware of this but it was entirely possible as he had been living out with the pony mares. Again, I was getting the feeling I was not hitting the mark. I asked him to tell me what he thought was wrong, and again he gave me the stomach feeling. By this time, Dave had ventured in and said to ask Merlin if anything hurt higher up. I posed the question and, although it was not pain, he kept making me swallow repeatedly. "Now you're on the right track", announced Dave, "ask some more!" I tried again but Merlin insisted on pointing out this stomach cramping, so then Dave said that maybe it had been something different from what he had thought! Sarah suggested I might as well look at him now and as soon as I did, this instantly explained the 'I am worth a lot less' statement, for he stood before me so thin with all his ribs showing as if to be counted.

We then had a discussion about what was happening, and the long and short of it was Merlin simply did not want to eat. Step in Bob, with his dental experience, that was one avenue that could be quickly explored and discounted and, as was the case, his teeth were fine. I asked why they had asked me to check higher up and what would the swallowing be about. It turned out this little stallion had had strangles (a serious and very contagious infection affecting the throat area) three years previously and had been left with scarring from it. Dave thought perhaps there was an increasing restriction, hence the swallowing action and the lack of will to eat. I begged to differ and said that I would ask Merlin what he thought. He told me that he was sure he had a stomach problem and actually pointed out where, which was an area directly in front of his sheath (male genital area). He then gave me a picture of a really inflamed-looking gut, like a hosepipe with the inside of it red, swollen and bulbous. With that, Dave said he would go and get his thermal imaging camera. "Thermal imaging camera?" I questioned.

"Yes, it shows up hot spots caused by inflammation."

Sarah got Merlin out of his stable and Dave set up this majorly expensive bit of equipment. Bob and I were like over-enthusiastic kids looking at the next generation of an XBox! Dave demonstrated how it clearly showed hot, normal and cold areas in a thermal image, like a heat x-ray. Dave by now was pointing this device, complete with a red laser beam, straight at the top of Merlin's off hind leg. Amazingly, it clearly showed a splash of red inflammation corresponding with a muscle mass, so that verified what I had said originally about there being a discomfort from some form of trauma caused by the 'undignified falling from grace!'

With bated breath, I watched as Dave lined the laser spot up to the area in front of the sheath, and heard him say, "Well I never, you can see, as clear as day, there is an obvious amount of heat in that area, so do you think he has ulcers?"

"Hang on", I replied, "I shall ask him." Merlin was quick to dispel that but said he felt his gut was inflamed and that when he ate, it made it worse and he felt sick. As horse people know, horses cannot vomit due to their physical make-up, but they can feel nauseous which then made us realise what all the swallowing was about. I did my usual, and asked the animal what he thought would help him and, quick as a flash, he volunteered that Dave had stomach powders that were really good!! BUT, then gave me a picture of someone struggling trying to get anything into his mouth that he really didn't like the taste of. I laughed and said to Sarah, "I think you might be struggling to get this down him, as I think he can be a 'little' resistant to be wormed etc.!" She smiled and nodded back in agreement.

We said our 'goodbyes' and wished them well and also the best of luck with Merlin. This stallion was in rocky waters because he was deteriorating so fast and they were really beginning to think it would maybe be kinder to send him to Heaven.

A couple of months later, I had a stand at a horse show and who should appear but Sarah! She smiled and thanked me and said, "To be honest, I had my doubts, but you were spot on (this use of phrase tickled me, thinking how apt as the thermal laser showed the 'spot') and you will be so pleased to hear that Merlin took his medicine, (albeit with his usual resistance!) and started eating the next day! He started to perk up and then quickly put weight on. He is now happily back out in the field with his mares. So, well done, you!"

I was absolutely delighted with the result and glad to have been of help using my communication ability to help save his life from being sadly shortened. Also having now seen a thermal camera first hand, I am able to tell others now that machines like this exist. They are brilliant; as they are non-invasive and painlessly 'picture' inside the body/limb and, hopefully, get to the root of a problem quickly before more damage occurs.

Months later Sarah sent me an email to let me know that one of her 16.2 mares had presented them with a surprise foal. It was tiny and the spitting image of Merlin! So she concluded; that although she had no idea how he got to her, with such a height difference this had to be something to do with the aforementioned 'fall from grace!'

A Close Shave

Jemma phoned me about her cat, Purdy, and said that there was a little mystery going on, and apparently I was the person to contact to solve it!

Purdy was a stunning long-haired exotic cat, whose colour I could describe as peach, although I am sure that would not be technically correct, but she had that 'blushed peach' look about her. She was about ten years old and came across like a genuinely happy cat, but…how on earth had she done 'that' to her head?

I asked Purdy to show me what Jemma was talking about and with that she showed me a wound on the top of her head. "That's it," confirmed Jemma, but how did she get it? I had a closer 'look' and it looked rather like a triangle, starting with the long edge at the front and the point heading backwards toward her ears.

"Mmm, rather an odd one," I agreed.

Jemma said, "The vet thought she had been bitten by a rat, but I couldn't see that myself." I totally agreed as there was no obvious sign of teeth marks and no depth to it. I described it more like a scrape, and Purdy assured us it wasn't sore and would heal very quickly.

To unravel this mystery was not just about the 'cut', but why was she now acting so oddly? Purdy 'took' me round the back of some stables and showed me a hay shelter, a lean-to type that was rather low with a corrugated tin roof covering it. Jemma said there was one round the back and that Purdy did spend time in there. Purdy expanded on the picture and showed it stacked up high with hay which, it turned out at that point, was full. Suddenly – 'thud' and a motion picture was running before my eyes. First the noise, then the sight of Purdy jumping up and running forward at the same time, but in the limited space, straight into the edge of a sheet of corrugated tin! This sharp edge created the triangle as she dipped her head down fast on contact, however it still managed to 'shave' her hair and skin, giving her a perfectly triangular-shaped abrasion! So that was one half of the mystery solved, but the other we still had to get to.

Purdy was usually quite a laid back cat, but she was acting like she was totally disconcerted by something that seemed to be between the hay store and the back door of the house and kept running back indoors.. I asked her to show me and she gave me a picture of a big black cat, rather feral looking, with fur sticking out – rather like the type you would see in a kid's cartoon.

I asked Jemma if she owned one of the same description and she did not. I asked Purdy to show him to me again and she obligingly gave me a picture of post and rails at the back of some stables, complete with this large cat sitting on them. These rails led to the side of the building and over to the lean-to, so now we deduced what had happened; whilst Purdy was having one of her well-earned cat naps, and was snuggled up comfortably in the hay when the big cat jumped down onto the tin roof. We told her that as scary as this black cat looked, with the noise and her panicking, the chances are he would have been scared too. We assured her that she could easily dash back into the house, should she see him again and with that she made us laugh, saying, "I think I maybe over-reacted and was a bit of a silly billy!!" We said we understood and not to be afraid, try to forget about it and start going back outside again. Jemma promised she would keep a close eye out for the scary cat too and will send him off if she sees him.

The strange thing is that Jemma asked around and nobody recognised this cat, and she had never seen it herself. Anyway, the next day Purdy trotted out again and went back to sleeping in the hay shed with all forgotten like it was just a bad dream. In the past two years, nobody had seen hide nor hair of the scary cat either and at least there have been no more disturbances or mishaps. That side of the mystery we will never know for sure but at least her head healed quickly and there were no scars to show for her little misadventure.

Beyond Logic

The minute I got this call, I knew it was going to be difficult and would emotionally challenge me to the hilt. I had been made aware, through the national news, that yet another thoroughly appalling case of cruelty had been uncovered. This was not involving a few helpless horses but a vast quantity, which beggar's belief how this was not spotted earlier. I personally refuse to look at the pictures and read any of the horrific stories (my husband kindly cuts them out of papers for me), as if I am not in a position to help, I am left bereft for these poor beings and their sufferance.

This case was brought to me by a girl whose horse I had chatted to previously who was a volunteer at this large rescue centre. Unbeknown to me they had organised a whip-round and booked me to talk to Cinders who, a year after she was found, was still totally shut down. I knew that this would be testing for all concerned and as an added pressure I was put on loud speaker so they could all hear and ask relevant questions.

Little Cinders was actually a well-bred broodmare and had shared the same 'hell-hole' with so many others. I do not use the word 'hell-hole' lightly, but if you saw what I did you would understand. The emotion and pain came searing into me, straight from her heart to mine. She had literally been living in what looked like a battlefield, with animals walking round the dead and dying, with emaciated rotting bodies sharing their prison. Their incarceration was by means of large corrugated barns, well off the beaten track, cold, wet, and stinking of all the disgusting aromas achieved by years of neglect.

She was literally bawling at me, "Why me, why me?" and this wasn't about, 'why did it happen to her', it was the familiar cry of someone that has survived, when so many perished. I freely admit, I sobbed my way through the beginning of this communication, as did many of the staff involved. I set about explaining to her that none of this was her fault, and that she maybe was 'chosen' to be strong enough to survive. There is no way, in the whole world, I could ever be able to explain why these despicable people did what they did, but rest assured, that you were the defenceless animals, and they were the barbaric perpetrators of such mindless cruelty.

She just cried and cried, which was heart rending, but at least (from her subconscious) she was showing emotion, as to this point in time, simply nobody had been able to get through to her. She then suddenly wailed, "My son, where is my son, is he alive or dead, where is he?" This took me aback, and I quickly reminded the girls that this was a 3-way (actually more like a 6-way) conversation and that Cinders would hear their reply. Much to my relief, her son had survived, and was with about a dozen youngsters, at another rescue centre, was very happy and having fun with the other boys. With this news, the relief I felt was immeasurable for the pair of us and I hoped this would help turn a corner. This question from her really taught me something and I hope that others, if they don't mind me saying, now may take this on board – if you were to change this situation to say, rescuing a load of women and children from a brutal cult, BUT, they were all *mute*, so therefore could not speak. You do this miraculous thing, and become their saviour, but space is limited where you can give them a safe house. You logically decide to put the grownups in one place and the children in a different, but more suitable, place. Can you see what would happen? Exactly the same as this little mare, the intolerable angst of not knowing what had happened to the one (or more) you love more than life itself, but have no voice to ask, to at least know that they are safe.

As Cinders had been a breeding mare, she knew this as her job, and still felt like something was expected of her, and had been very unsure what. This was whether she would have to be ridden, she had no idea of what this actually entailed, and if she didn't have work to do, then she presumed that she would be surplus to requirements. So, she was existing from day to day, wondering if 'that day' was to come, like she had seen so many go before her. We set out to explain to her that she owed the world nothing, simply nothing, and the centre wanted to care for her for the rest of her days. As much as we tried to explain this, she would not have it, she had this in-built desire to feel worthy, but felt the only way to achieve this was to do something to earn her keep, so to speak. By this time, her emotional state had subsided, and she was talking quite rationally. She knew that she would not have any more babies, but with her experience, 'What a good nanny she would make!!' She carried on chatting and even told us who she wished to 'nanny', and showed me a group of Falabellas (miniature ponies). The staff laughed, and gasped at the same time, because from Cinder's stable she could see the small group in the distance! They were well known for causing a bit of a rumpus, so a mature lady would be just the answer to teach them some manners and respect. I do seem to spend my time saying, 'I can't promise he or she will change', but I did feel so much lighter in my heart and could only hope that this communication would do for her what it has done for so many other abused animals. Cinders listened to me and suddenly speculated, "Actually, I think I could be quite cheeky and would really like to go down the field and have a little buck!!" Well, this took us all aback, as this little girl was being led out to the paddock, with no self-will, and not even enough sparkle to try a little canter. I said to just note it down, and if it happened, savour the moment, as I am sure she would.

I finished the call, and having found out about the whip-round, tried to insist on non-payment, but they said they were more than grateful, so I surrendered. After the call, I did some emotional healing for her. I asked her to imagine unloading all her bad memories into my hands, which she did, picture by picture, and feeling by feeling. When she had run out of all that was trapped in her heart, I got her to look to the sky, and watch it all blow away in the wind, disappearing so it could never to return. In simplistic terms, I would say it is like deleting computer files in the recycle bin, and hearing that 'scrunch' as they disappear, never to be retrieved.

The next day, my phone bleeped with a text, I opened it and melted with emotion as I read: "Just to let you know, Cinders is so much happier today, thank you so very much!" I have had updates since, and yes, she did have her buck, and is going from strength to strength!

As distressing as this case was to do, I was hugely grateful to Cinders for trusting me, and those around her, but also for teaching us such a valuable lesson. Rescue situations sometimes do involve family separations; they don't have a voice to ask about their kin, so please reassure them by telling them what you, yourself, would want to know.

Animal Magic

There are some things in life you just find yourself agreeing to and when the occasion arises, you instinctively think, "How on earth did I get into this?" This was most certainly one of those occasions.

Early one Monday morning my dear friend Jay, who lives in North Wales, phoned me and started with one of those classic lines, "You can say no, BUT… on Friday the local hotel is having a psychic night, but the psychic has been in an accident and can't make it. My first thought, was YOU!!" I knew exactly which hotel it was, as we had been there previously for a group meal after a holistic fair I had been working at. Jay went on to explain that she thought it would be such fun, and as she knew I had done public fundraisers, would I be willing to step into the breach? My brain engaged for a whole two seconds and I agreed to help, as, if nothing else, it would be lovely to go and stay with her and have a good old catch up. Although she had explained to the manager what I did, she said she would pass my details to him so he could contact me directly.

The email duly arrived within the hour, giving the time they expected me to 'entertain' for, and a request about my terms of payment. I replied, on my usual email, complete with signature of my web address and asked that a donation be given for my cancer charity. That was the last I heard and, by the time the Friday came, Jay and I were rather nervously excited but also rather confused as she had been to the hotel during the week and there were still adverts for the psychic gentleman, but nothing regarding me. She spoke with one of the receptionists who, at that point was standing beside the hotel parrot, an African Grey named Alfie, which prompted Jay to recall an hilarious chat we had with him a few months previous. This occurred at the end of a group evening as we were all gathering in the foyer to leave, when some bright spark suggested that I could have a 'chat' with the parrot. He was thoroughly engaging, and would squawk in acknowledgment with various things he told me as I announced them to his personal audience. He also informed us that, "People bark at me like a dog!" How indignant was that, and what did they expect him to do, bark back? Well, he refused to lower himself to their games, so would just cock his head to the side and act confused or as dull as the person barking! I asked him if he had anything else that he thought would be of interest to tell us before we left, and he laughingly informed us, "Someone sleeps at this desk, you know!" We chortled and thought how funny that he was watching this person passing the hours sleeping instead of working!! So, this was three months later, and we now knew that the sleeping secret had become apparent, courtesy of some newly installed hotel CCTV!

On the Friday, with the sun shining on this beautiful crisp autumn day, I set off for my two hour journey, laden with flowers for Jay and a whacky idea of how to make the evening a bit more entertaining than just talking with people's animals. I normally have a lovely time; people tend to have photos of their pets on their phones, so I have a look at their picture and then start the chat. I always explain that it is best to chat to happy/cheeky/cute animals as a public forum is not the place to bring up emotionally disturbed or very sick animals.

I had arranged with Jay to meet at the hotel and, typically, the heavens had opened, so even running into the hotel, my hair that I had spent time preening, was considerably flattened, but my spirits weren't...well, not at that point anyway! Jay introduced me to the owner, a little northern lady, who admitted to not having held one of these events before. Accompanied by the manager also, we were shown to the room and were slightly confused by the table and chairs set up: it looked like a dining room, to all intents and purpose. I explained that usually just rows of chairs for the audience are required and then I ask the person, whose animal is chosen, to come out and sit at the front adjacent to the audience.

"What animals?" the manager said questioningly.

"Oh don't worry, they won't actually bring animals here, I will do it from a photo or description only."

"I still don't see where the animals fit in," the owner said.

"Err, hang on..." I stammered, "what type of thing do you think I am doing tonight?"

She replied with a muffled voice and an arm pointed to the sky effect, "Well...talking to them, up there?" her voice tightening with every sentence.

"Ahh, no," I ventured, "I talk to animals down here, err, that was not what you were expecting, was it?" I quickly turned to the manager and asked him, "Did you check out my website on my email?"

"Oh yes," he replied.

"And what was it about?"

"Err, animals!" But he had clearly forgotten to pass this information on.

"Oh dear," the owner stated, "we have sold about sixty tickets for a psychic show, and you are doing animals!"

I asked her if she still wanted me to go ahead, which she did, but I suggested that if anyone wanted their money back then I would think that would be fair under the circumstances. Then, on a lighter note, added, "Could I borrow your parrot for the second half?"

"Yes, by all means, but what for?"

I quickly repeated the previous parrot chat and she thought it was a fun idea but did warn me about his choice use of language.

I didn't really have a chance to be nervous, by this time I had nothing to lose, as most of the people turning up were in for a bit of a surprise anyway, so I figured it could not get any worse. I did the first half and chatted to four different animals, and at least managed to prove that what I do is real, although obviously it was not everyone in the audience's cup of tea. During the break, several rather disgruntled people left and I apologised to the others, but said that we would borrow Alfie the parrot and attempt to do some clairvoyant work instead. I came up with the concept that people would introduce themselves to him, and he would try to tell them something interesting he thought they would like to hear about themselves. I was quick to absolve myself of any responsibility and said, "If this goes wrong, you can blame Alfie, and if this goes right, you can tell him how clever he is!"

The first willing participant stood up, who was heavily pregnant, so I had a laugh and said, "Oh, he say's you are having a baby!" and with perfect timing, Alfie laughed like a drain.

She duly came to the front, and as I directed her, Alfie chimed in with the odd, "Right," and, "Hello," and "Okay," all in the right places, and at this point I thought all was going smoothly.

I then posed the question to him, "Alfie, what would you like to say to the lady?" A few thoughtful seconds elapsed, and then, "**** Off!!" which was clearly heard!! Well, the audience erupted and fell about in hysterics, much to Alfie's delight shown by his screeching laughter. I carried on (eventually) and he managed to mis-direct me, by giving me wrong information, and then just at the moment of me saying it, he would give an elongated, "Nooo", and cause even more laughter. He did actually redeem himself (and me) by giving me some accurate information about someone changing their job, another being 'secretly' impatient, and a man taking his shoes off without bothering to untie the laces!

The hotel owner was extremely generous, and gave me £100 for my cancer charity. I even had people come up and thank me for introducing them to the world of animal communication, something they had no idea even existed. And as for Alfie, his performance is now legendary in his hometown. I am sure the staff will be ever so polite to him and work ever so hard in his presence! As the evening was being filmed by Jay's husband, Kim, there is now a clip out there in cyber space for many to view, showing an evening that I don't think Alfie will ever forget, and neither will I.

"They do wet and cold - I don't!"
A collie explaining why he refused to be trained as a working sheepdog!

"I know, I know, when I do get silly, this leads to our inconsequential differences!"
A horse that really is a 'two strides forward and three strides back', with a very sympathetic owner who really is struggling to get him to concentrate on the job in hand.

"I'm a dark horse you know!"
A horse trying to impress on us his prowess as a showjumper and maybe didn't realise he was actually grey!

"I'm like Benny Hill, but with a skirt on!"
A very funny female cat describing herself!

Out of Step

After one of my charity evenings at a country pub, having proved that what I do is not pie in the sky, a lady approached me and said she would love me to talk to her mare. I gave her a card and said I looked forward to chatting with them both. As is so often the case, I hear nothing for months and then, when the timing is right, they get in touch with me.

Lianne is a lady that really knows about horses and runs a large equestrian yard. This particular mare she had bred herself and was nine years old. Jinty was a good sixteen hands, of show-jumping bloodlines, and physically, had turned out to be exactly what Lianne had hoped for. What her owner hadn't hoped for was the temperament difficulties, which is why she had come to me as a last gasp! I have to mention at this point, I just love the use of the word 'temperamental' as it's so true: it's half temper, half mental, so pretty self explanatory!!

I tuned in with Jinty and was immediately given the impression of a child stamping its feet and screwing up its face! This was actually a fair description as she kicks seven bells out of her stable walls and pulls those faces that could curdle milk. She started to rant that 'oh life just seemed so unfair', and 'why didn't Lianne want her?' Well, that second question threw us both as she was homebred and her owner wanted to help her, not sell her. I explained this and let her carry on so she took that opportunity to inform us that she also knew she was all that Lianne had ever wanted! This was the truth, in fact, she was the first horse Lianne had bred and she was highly delighted to see how this mare had physically matured into this attractive and very athletic horse. Jinty then interrupted with; "I couldn't be bothered with them though," combined with a picture of a couple of foals. I passed this comment and picture over, expecting to hear that she had been a broodmare but not amused with the motherhood. Actually, they were not her foals but her own younger brothers! One born the year following her birth and the other the year after that, and she really did resent them, which had become perfectly apparent to Lianne. It was assumed that she was of a bossy nature which is why she pushed them about and, although not nasty in a dangerous way, made it very clear that she wanted very little to do with them, and they were to get out of her way when asked. This was quite strange really as most youngsters tend to get along, especially siblings, but never mind, there was no harm done and, in the end she lived in a field away from them.

I started to feel very uncomfortable in what would be Jinty's off hind leg (right hind) and this was the reason for the call now. As I mentioned, she does kick her stable walls with vengeance and had apparently now made that leg sore, so what could I do to help to stop her doing this? I did comment to Lianne that it was quite 'far down the line', as she has been doing this for years now, but I would try to find out where this resentment had come from. She now was giving me an ache in both hocks, so I acknowledged it and went back to the anger issue.

I thought I would ask Jinty her good points and see where that would lead us. She straightaway volunteered what a great jumper she was, although rather inconsistent. This was so true; she was an extremely talented show-jumper but would just sometimes throw the towel in, as if she had lost interest. Then she asked a similar question like the one earlier, "Why does she not want to ride me?" I asked Lianne if that question made any sense, and it did. It transpired that other people competed her, not Lianne, as she felt she wasn't a good enough rider to do her justice and really was not up to jumping at that level. "But I wanted to do it for her not for them," was the sad comment passed by Jinty.

"Please go on", I urged the mare.

"She told me I was all she ever wanted, then she had the boys, then gives me to everyone else to ride! When she occasionally rides me, I am far quieter for her - I try to be good." With that outpouring, I said to Lianne that it made me think that this little mare really felt like her nose had been put out of joint and had misconstrued what actually was just a practicality.

At last, we could see where all the anguish and temper had come from and why Jinty would demand attention by bashing the walls and pulling faces as she, in her own confused way, felt rejected. Firstly, her owner had bred another two horses so, on principle, she obviously was not enough for her and, secondly, her owner got other people to compete her so she was probably not good enough for her Lianne to want to compete! This inferiority complex was completely of her own making but there are some people like that too; like a person sees someone whisper something to someone else and they automatically assume it is something about them. As we know, most of the time it is not; it is their own *assumption*, not fact and that can cause so many misunderstandings.

Lianne was actually quite dismayed with all that she had heard, but said it had just never crossed her mind and what could we do to try and help her? I logically explained to this rather confused horse that it was really a misunderstanding on her part and the fact that, "Just because your owner is breeding more horses, it is not to replace you or because you are not up to standard, it is just the way life is." I also told her that she was so right in thinking Lianne had said she was all that she could have wanted, it was absolutely true and that had not changed. I sensed that feeling of a 'sigh of relief' and asked her to tell me her favourite sign of love/attention. I always ask this from every animal, whether it be the stroking of a horse's forehead or a dog having its tummy rubbed, because once they have told you and you do it, they know you do it realising how much it means to them. This is similar to giving a child their favourite meal if they have done something really good, or just simply because you want to. So, this 'reward' for an animal is good to know and used in the right situations can really pay dividends.

We finished the chat and Lianne said she would go and have a personal one-to-one talk with Jinty and said they would get the vet to check her hocks too. Within the month, Lianne came back to me, and, although Jinty still kicks the stable, even other people on the yard have noticed it is done much less frequently. Her outlook is far more relaxed and her owner is going to try and watch her being competed (like a parent watching a child), also she is now on a supplement for her hocks and moving easier. I don't think this mare will ever fully stop her kicking habit but, as time goes on, and the 'logical' takes over the rather 'illogical' I think she will find life a lot more tolerable, as will Lianne.

Personally Speaking

Jane, a girl in her late teens, contacted me as I had chatted to a horse on the yard she was working at. This chat was actually to be with her cat, not a horse, and the reading turned into one of those lovely personal, intuitive ones.

All my work is guided and translated by my own spirit guide, Rolf, a cat that I never knew down here on earth but he wanted to work with me and has 'shown' me things all my life. I just did not recognise it as clairvoyance, or whatever you wish to call it. Sometimes, one that we know and love goes to Heaven and will then become a guide for us,. But, more often than not, it is either a person or animal that is a complete stranger, who had actually been watching over you all your life. It is them that give you that 'gut feeling' so please try and pay attention to it as, you never know, it might save you saying that familiar line, 'I just knew there was something not right about that!' I, like many, can hear and speak to spirits and although it took me a bit of getting used to, it is often too much for others to understand. I do not try to push my views onto people but am in the fortunate position to be able to prove what I do is real.

I was talking with a vet recently who is into homeopathy, which again is a difficult one to 'scientifically prove' as you are taking quantities diluted sometimes up to a thousand times, and it works? I actually have had great results with homeopathy as I bet many of you have too. This vet was doing a talk on the subject and a group of people were shaking their heads with that attitude of 'complete poppycock' about them. This vet decided to ask one of them if they minded answering a question that might help scientifically clarify things, so of course 'Mr Bumptious' was more than ready to defend 'logic' corner.

"Have you ever been in love?" asks the vet.

"Of course I have!" replied Mr Bumptious.

"Are you absolutely sure?" the vet questioned again.

"Of course I am, man!" he replied emphatically.

"Okay then, scientifically prove it!" replied the vet. So with that brilliant line the conversation ended and 'Mr Bumptious' sat down and proceeded to listen politely to the rest of the talk.

I love that example and now quite often use it myself, and it does tend to make people slightly less judgemental when I then proceed to prove what I know to be real. With healing, homeopathy, acupuncture, and many alternative ways, there will always be that excuse for doubting clarified by the, 'Well it might have got better on its own', or, "It was such a coincidence!" But in a way I am very lucky that I can prove what I do, there and then, at that precise time. When I tune into an animal the first thing I do is to ask them to tell me something about themselves and I repeat it to their owners to validate that it sounds like their animal and, if a bit vague, I will ask for more. What they say gives you a good indication of their personality straightaway as some will say how gentle and thoughtful they are and others can be very boastful and 'full on!' If you can imagine having, say, ten photos of people put in front of you and then you try to 'guess' their personalities. To get a hundred percent correct would take some doing, so when I stand up in front of people and describe their animal's personality and then start to tell them things that are totally relevant to that particular animal, even sceptics will find it hard to argue with that. Luck would only carry a fake so far and, anyway, people are quick to spread bad news as fast as good, so this works in my favour. I trust my guides to give me the right information I know that they will not make me say or do anything improper. I am working for all the reasons that are good; to help not hinder and to bring relief in whichever form it comes in but, most of all, to be honest and true to myself and to simply try to do my best.

Jane's cat, Chantelle, immediately said that she was unhappy, unsettled and thought they should go home! She was very sweet but straight to the point as she thought Jane, herself, was unhappy too! I thought carefully about how I was to put this over and asked Jane, "Is this a temporary arrangement where you are living now?"

"Well, yes and no!" was her reply. "To be honest I had moved here about five months ago but Chantelle has not settled and I do not know what to do for the best." Chantelle immediately turned the conversation round to Jane's life and choices and informed me that Jane was 'surviving' not 'living'. It had quickly become apparent that the reason for this reading coming to me was not really for the cat but for her owner and, although I avoid reading people, this situation didn't faze me as it was just meant to be, via her cat. I asked Jane if she minded me giving over this personal information and she said, "No, it will all help I'm sure, although I never expected it to be about me, but it's great, if you don't mind, thank you." I then told her the 'surviving' bit and she said that was the problem, she had moved away, quite far from home and it hadn't worked out how she had hoped and was really struggling.

Chantelle then said, "She is not eating properly either!" sounding like a 'mother hen', strange from a cat, eh? But, again, this was correct as she had been living on sausage rolls etc. because she was working all hours possible and so they were quick and pretty cheap.

Jane got into the swing of Chantelle trying to sort out her life for her and said to ask her if she should really go back home? There was no pause from her cat who announced, "It would be far better for both of us as we are loved there and it would be much warmer! Also, she could study aromatherapy there too!" Jane told me that in the past she had thought about learning aromatherapy, but it had never really been much more than a passing thought.

"What about the book then?" said Chantelle.

So I asked Jane, "Do you not have a book about it?"

"No, I don't think so," she replied, but then Chantelle showed me a book with a purple cover, so I asked what that was about, and Jane said, "I don't know, err, a purple cover? Oh yes, I glanced through it the other day as I was looking for something to help with period pains, and, oh yes, it was about aromatherapy. Oh how funny, I hadn't even twigged what you were talking about!" Chantelle then, just to show off, told us that when Jane was studying for her present job she had kept losing her books, and suggested that she kept them all in one place as that would have made life easier for her! Jane laughed, and said that was just 'so her!'

I was enjoying this chat and it was nice for a change to use my gift to help this young girl, and it did! She decided, there and then, that she would hand in her notice and move back home, much to Chantelle's relief. She said this had also ignited her interest in aromatherapy and realised that it was something she could study part-time so could still work to pay her way. Although the study and holistic work she was doing with the horses was what she wanted to do, the move had made her and her cat's life a misery. So, on a positive note, she had at least gained six months experience under her belt and she felt sure she could find something similar but nearer to her friends and family. Jane thought maybe at a later date, she could try moving to another location but would take a lot more into consideration before doing it!

A Promise Kept

As word spreads about animal communication it has been hugely endorsed by those who have had personal experience of its accuracy. In *Animal Insight* there was a very sad story – Bamboozled – in which a little mare showed me a problem in her neck vertebrae and eventually went to Heaven. Her owner, Meg, passed my name on to her friend, Ann, who was really struggling with her mare whom she had owned for four years.

Connie was a big strapping mare and just completely full of attitude. She was now nine years old and since the day Ann had owned her had acted like she resented everyone and everything. As usual, I knew nothing about her when the reading started but was to quickly establish that she was angry and had no respect or care for Ann at all. I felt very sorry for Ann having to listen to the rantings from her horse that she had desperately tried to get through to, but, sadly, had failed. I explained that this was just like a child having counselling, I am here to listen and let them give it from their point of view and then start the mending process. We both knew that this would be very difficult, if not impossible, as constantly during the past four years Ann had borne witness to Connie's temper and now we had to try and see if we could undo anything, or maybe to find out that this was just her.

I told Connie that I was here to help her, not judge her, and anything she wanted to tell me would be fine, just please trust me. Immediately I was greeted with, "It won't make any difference, there is no point!"

"What do you mean by that?" I asked back.

"I tried before and failed, whatever I did wasn't good enough, so it is not worth trying okay?!!" Mmm, angry really was the best description, but I asked her to carry on. "Oh, it's not just her, it is everyone. I just don't want to know...there is no point. We try, you know, but are just not good enough, and never will be!"

I repeated this all back to Ann, and she said that she reckoned this was about her past as a show jumper. Apparently she had been good, but not good enough to get up to the higher grades required of the professional yard she had been brought from. This made sense to me, and it is not the first time I have had this scenario. If you were to put it into human terms: when you had tried your heart out, whether it be in a relationship or a workplace, and someone lets you know you were simply not good enough, you would be deeply hurt. This would be totally understandable as, in any type of relationship, you have invested your time and trust and you can feel betrayed even though it wasn't meant in that way. We, as people, are not sold on to solve a problem, but animals, especially horses, are.

Connie freely admitted to me she had her 'barriers up' and that, to her, was the safest way to stay. I chatted away to her and asked her if she really wanted to do without love in her life? She paused and said she had done 'love' before and didn't want to risk getting hurt again. I explained that Ann had kept her for four whole years in spite of her attitude, and not being the easiest of rides either. She then said she had been 'sent away'! According to Ann, that was only for schooling but Connie had come back fairly quickly as this didn't go well either. "So, Connie", I said, "you have heard the truth from me, and have also heard what Ann has said too, so do you not think it is time to take a chance and give her a break?"

Connie paused and drew breath, "I can't promise, but I will think about it, okay?"

"Yes" I replied, "You really could have a home for life you know, but the ball is firmly in your court from now on."

"Okay", she ventured, "I want to try!"

I was quite taken aback by this admission and said to Ann, "I don't want to get your hopes up, but she says she wants to try so I am going to ask her what you could say to help her keep her word."

Connie heard and answered, "Enough is enough!" Well that was straight to the point, so it was agreed that at the point of poor behaviour she would be reminded of this conversation by her own choice of words.

We covered various other points, like the 'loading' issue. Now this was actually quite an obvious one, as she had loaded well to go to the schooling yard and back again. Her fear was a logical one, she was really not happy there and so when Ann tried to load her, she just presumed that she was being loaded to go for more schooling, or being shipped off elsewhere. We reassured her that this would not happen and so to please try and trust Ann's judgement and to take the Rescue Remedy that you, yourself Connie have recommended! On the subject of Rescue Remedy, again, it is one that people are likely to say it couldn't possibly work; after all, it is a dilute form of a flower essence! All I can say is that I have had many animals ask for it and it has done the trick, from travelling worries, riding a dressage test to even a dog being car-sick! Again, it won't work for everyone but it is well worth a try, and for a nervous rider on a nervous horse, often a dose for both rider and horse will help psychologically, if nothing else!

I finished the call and commended Ann for her patience, and asked her to thank Meg for putting her in touch with me and hoped that we had made a break-through, but only time would tell.

A few months went by and Ann booked me for another session. I did what I usually do, and re-introduced myself to Connie and asked if anything had changed since we last spoke. Much to my surprise/relief she sounded so much calmer and seemed to be happy. So gingerly I put it to Ann by saying, "Well, to me, she seems happier and wanting to talk rather than shout!"

"Oh yes, she is much happier, she is a different horse!"

I was lost for words (which for me is a miracle!) but asked Ann to expand on what had changed, and was interrupted by Connie with, "I am even doing a bit of affection," which, again, Ann confirmed. At that point I took the opportunity to ask her favourite sign of affection which turned out to be having the front of her head rubbed, and not gently-gently, but with real conviction! Ann had even loaded her and said how good she was and again Connie butted in with, "Rescue Remedy is great!!" Well, we laughed and laughed, firstly, at the fact of her seemingly 'patting herself on her back' with the original suggestion, and, secondly, at this horse who had been so angry a few months ago but now was showing us her sense of humour.

Now Connie had the art of this 'chatting' she also impressed upon me a few physical problems she had. Ann noted them and said that she would get her looked at. I was, as was Ann, overjoyed at this result. I have talked to her four times overall and I could not finish this story without saying how sweet this mare had become.

Connie also said to me, about herself, "I am glad to know I am a better person, I had just hidden 'me' away!" And, to me personally as the communicator, she said, "You made me a promise, and it was true!" I will never forget her saying that to me, those words still melt my heart to this day.

Finding the Key

In September 2009 I was sitting facing the entrance door at a holistic fair in Llangollen (North Wales) which I had worked at previously in March. I really do very few of the 'mind, body, spirit' type fairs but going there is more like a friends reunion and full of good atmosphere. It also is a great excuse to get the caravan out, and walk our dog Sally over the many beautiful hills around there. Many people think that these sorts of fairs are full of 'strange' people reading cards and fortune-telling. Yes, of course there are people that do clairvoyant and psychic work (it is certainly not 'strange' to me, after all, I am clairvoyant too and most people are embracing what I do!) but also there are many healing and alternative types of treatments and much more there to experience. The great thing about these types of venues is that therapists tend to do taster sessions of what service they provide. So, for a small price you can decide for yourself what you think is beneficial or not. Now surrounded by many interesting people I was organised with my table all set up ready so that people could sit down and have an animal reading.

It was about ten o'clock when a girl walked through the doorway and her face did one of those double take impressions then blurted out, "I saw you on TV yesterday!" which made me laugh out loud as it was such a surreal moment. I am just an everyday ordinary person who just happens to have been extremely lucky how my life has transformed. "I just knew I had to come today, I just knew it, and when I saw you on TV I just knew you were the lady to help Ruby!" She burbled away at about a hundred miles an hour telling me, "I am not from round here; I am from Yorkshire and am just here to visit some friends. Wow, how amazing is this?!" I smiled and asked her and her friend, Lindsay, to take a seat.

Once Kirsty had got her breath back, and the look of shock had gone from her face, she sat down and introduced herself properly. She was only young (well comparative to me); I would hazard a guess at about twenty-five. She had travelled down with Lindsay from 'up North' where they share a flat and the dog in question, Ruby.

Ruby was a large female Doberman they had got from an animal rescue shelter about a year ago. I looked at a picture of her which Kirsty had on her mobile phone. I tuned in with Ruby and she immediately told me how loving she was but was very, very wary of strangers and men in particular. She started 'throwing' me pictures of what looked like some horrible, domineering person bawling and aggressively pushing her about, and then gave me a picture of what looked like her following round the walls inside a house. I asked the girls if she maybe did that inside the flat, like she was trying to look invisible, like blending into the walls. They recognised this instantly but said that was when they first got her and that she rarely does it now. Ruby then gave a completely opposite style of picture and this was of her lying fully stretched out over someone on a settee! They laughed as this was so right but being a big dog they couldn't let her do it for long as she just totally squashed them, but it was such fun! Doberman dogs are big and strong and often weigh the same as a small person, so I totally understood why this affection-seeking mode had its limitations!

We covered various problems but the main one was beating their logical brains: "Why, when Lindsay went out, did Ruby not bark or get upset, yet when Kirsty went out she would not settle and would bark and whine until Kirsty returned?"

"Mmm," I thought, "this will be interesting," so I simply asked Ruby what was the difference about Lindsay going out and Kirsty doing the same?

"But she might not come back," was the worrying cry and I asked her to try and be clearer. Then she showed me a key and tried to get over to me that when the door wasn't locked that was the difference! I was not really sure I was picking this up correctly but passed it over anyway. Kirsty and Lindsay discussed the locking process to see if we could make sense of what she was saying. They established that Lindsay went out to work early in the mornings for her day job and would simply lock the door and go. Also, during the day if Kirsty went out she would lock up behind her too. On the other hand, when Kirsty went to her part-time job in the evening, Kirsty would seldom have to lock the door as Lindsay was at home.

With that, Kirsty's eyes widened, and she exclaimed, "Oh no, I hardly ever take my keys, because I don't need to unlock the door to come back in!" Now this was starting to make sense. Logically, if you were not coming back to a house, why would you take your keys with you? Bingo! We had got it, and now I had to explain this to Ruby and ask what Kirsty could do to help re-assure her. Very simply she asked that every time Kirsty went out to show Ruby her keyring, complete with the small stuffed toy that she visualised for me, and say, "Look, I have my keys, so I will be coming back."

We finished the chat and I said it was lovely to meet them and I hoped that Ruby would settle down. I got an update a few months later letting me know that although she was still barking, it was so much less and they could cope with it and hoped eventually it would peter out. Kirsty also said that it had made a huge difference to her and Lindsay just to hear what Ruby had to say and was so glad to have been guided in my direction. It had been such a special day for them, and I laughed about the 'TV recognition' which although was still surreal, made it an extra special one for me too!

Getting the Needle

A few years ago I met Jean who was teamed up with me on the animal communication course I attended. I still can picture the first thing I 'saw' and although she didn't pursue the communication side, we have not lost touch. Jean is qualified in many alternative treatments like Reiki and such like and has referred quite a few of her clients to me.

Teddy was one of them and owned by a sweet and kind person, Linda. She contacted me after getting Jean to look at Teddy, who then suggested the communication route might well be worth exploring. Linda had now owned him for eighteen months and he had not been properly sound for any of it and nobody could work out why.

Teddy's breeding was Warmblood and these horses are usually bred for dressage, but Teddy didn't move or even look like a dressage horse in any shape or form. He was such a lovely horse, so genuine, but was obviously uncomfortable and, hence, rather unwilling to carry himself in the way Linda would have liked.

He seemed to immediately recognise this communication was his chance to get his views over and started off straightaway with, "The problem is not in my feet!" That was a very bold statement as we hadn't even chatted about the niceties in his life, but as he decided to go straight to the medical, who was I to stop him. Far be it for me to contradict a vet's or farrier's opinion, so I had to carefully ascertain if there had been a mention of foot problems.

"Oh yes, he had bar shoes on!" (These are a special type of shoe, sort of like a full circle shape to support the whole foot) "Why do you ask?"

I thought the easiest thing to do was to repeat his words and see what she thought. I did, and she said she had wondered the same as she was not totally convinced this was a foot problem at all, but you have to listen to the advice you have been given. "How about, I ask him where he thinks the problem lies, if it is not his feet?" I suggested.

So I put that very question to him, and he stated, "It's in my withers!" (This is the area at the front of the saddle region) And not just that, he told us he thought he had got trapped nerves. He then showed me his conformation, he looked slightly croup high; this is when a horse is higher at the backend than they should be, so their back runs slightly downhill. This, you might think, is merely aesthetic, but although it would get you marked down in a showing class the problem is that often they require very expert saddlery as the natural downhill slope increases the pressure at the front end of the saddle. So if you have a horse of this build (it is far more common in Thoroughbreds) and you find they put the 'handbrake' on, especially when being ridden downhill, have a look at how your saddle does actually sit on him or her.

Linda said the wither area had been remarked on by Jean, but it was difficult because people just kept saying it was due to the feet. Teddy chimed in with, "Well, have the shoes made any difference?"

After a quick pause, "No," came Linda's reply, coupled with the comment that they had been costing her an arm and a leg! And for anyone that has had remedial shoeing done, you will know exactly where she is coming from. Not only are these bar shoes far more expensive, but the horses will be done probably more often, so you are paying vast sums out every six weeks at the least!

I 'scanned' over Teddy's body and it looked like he had one foot bigger than the other and also his right shoulder was more muscled than his left. He did not give me a 'painful' feeling, but just a general discomfort all over, and made me feel like I really wanted to keep dipping my back. As Teddy had held court for most of the conversation I asked him what he thought would help him, and without a pause he said, "Acupuncture!"

"Okay," I replied and then asked Linda if he had previously had acupuncture. He hadn't and she didn't even know of a practitioner that did it on people, let alone horses. I explained that it seemed that vets are the only people allowed to treat animals and maybe to ask Jean if she knew of one.

With his physical problems covered we chatted away about the nicer things in life, and he was a truly sweet horse. He really did not want to disappoint Linda, but was hoping that his body would get mended. We were aware by now that he had come to her like this so it might take quite a long time to undo everything but I wished them well and she promised to let me know how they got on.

Two months later, Linda emailed me asking me for an update chat with Teddy. I was delighted to hear from her and wondered how things had gone. Well, Teddy was so much brighter and expressing how much better and looser he felt. This was great news, and Linda said she was delighted with his progress and that the acupuncture really had seemed to have made a big difference. I asked out of interest if Jean had been able to recommend the vet, but this was not the case and Linda had managed to find one herself. Linda then told me this delightful tale, and this is how the conversation went:

To the receptionist, "Hello, I hear you have a vet that does acupuncture, is that correct?"

"Yes," came the reply, "would you like a word?"

"Yes please."

The vet: "How can I help you?"

"Yes," responds Linda, "I would like you to do some acupuncture on my horse please."

"Who is referring him?" the vet asked.

"Himself!" Linda replied.

"Himself?" the vet queried.

"Yes, the horse," Linda bravely replied and then explained, "This might sound mad to you but my horse has told an animal communicator he wants acupuncture, and where he wants it!!"

The vet paused then simply said, "Okay, if that is what he wants, then that is what he shall get," with a slightly bemused tone, but fortunately having the grace and decency to hear Linda out.

Linda arranged it all and Teddy saw the vet, and her very, very long needles! The vet trotted him up and down and could see he was unsound, so started the treatment. As sore as he was he tolerated it (just) and the wither area was treated as the vet picked up the sensitivity and lack of energy flow both sides. People that have experience of acupuncture know that sometimes the needles are put in elsewhere from the actual problem, as different points correspond to different parts. This update chat was now after Teddy's third treatment and incredibly he was sound! Teddy made us laugh, with this line, "Even the vet was gobsmacked!" but then so was I, as it turned out he had gone sound within two days of the first treatment! Incredibly this horse had been 'not right' for all this time and this was what acupuncture could achieve?!? The other astonishing thing was, that because Teddy was so 'wrong' the needles were actually getting pushed back up out of his rigid muscles and coming out bent at all different angles! On the next treatment they decided to sedate him, as this was not a comfortable experience. By the end of the fourth treatment, he was so much more relaxed and only required a little sedation. The vet left her needles in for longer this time and, on removal, there was not a bent one amongst them.

Teddy talked away and noted how much taller he seemed, Linda laughed and said she thought this too, and had it confirmed when the vet, who used to be able to reach up and get the needles out of his rump by standing on her tip toes, on the last treatment she had to find something to stand on. At last, Teddy was sound and holding himself properly and was even hacking out. This brought something to the fore, his stride had lengthened somewhat and he knew he felt like a different and much faster horse. He asked me so sweetly to tell Linda not to worry; he was still the same Teddy!

I was so pleased to help with this case, apart from the main aim to get Teddy fixed, but Linda was such a smashing owner and admitted that she had felt 'rather silly' telling the vet he had 'referred himself'. But that was the truth, and spoke volumes for her belief in my type of work. It also certainly gave the vet an excellent example of what communication can achieve, and that animals can really ask for their own treatment, and often one that works at that!

Linda was so kind to write out extra notes to help me get the facts right in this story and finished her letter with (I quote): 'So Jackie, I can't thank you enough for giving us both back the will to live. Keep up your fantastic vocation.' Signed off with: Linda and Teddy xx and a soft whicker!

FEED
FARRIER
VET
© JAcks 2010

A Worrying Case

It was a week before Christmas and I was contacted by David who had heard of me through a friend of a friend. Although he did not ask for a reading, or even mention it, he gave me the outline of the serious problem that was occurring between his dogs.

David and his wife, Sue, lived down South with their two Harlequin Great Danes, Rufus (nearly nine) and Tom who is rather younger at two. David explained that they had kept two entire (uncastrated) males together for years. He said that his last dog was called Boston, who had passed over in 2006, and there had never been any problems between him and Rufus. Having kept Harlequin Danes (these are white with black 'torn' patches distributed over their entire body) for over thirty years, they could not understand what was going so wrong.

As I said, he didn't specifically ask for a reading but gave me the lovely line wondering if I could help them by 'remote control'! That conjured up a lovely picture of someone just pointing a TV remote and, as if by magic, this 'wand' would cure the problem instantaneously!

The long and short of the story was that the young dog, Tom, had grown up and become the dominant one and had actually attacked Rufus. David and Sue had decided to ask the vet to 'chemically' castrate him to see if this would improve things. It worked, and peace was restored and the two dogs acted like great mates. But, just before Christmas, which was about six months after the injection, it had obviously worn off as Tom had been aggressive towards Rufus again. Tom had another injection and, for some reason, this time Rufus would not leave him alone. It sounded like Tom had had enough as he had now retaliated and bitten Rufus on the leg. These two dogs were now being kept separately and it was a very uneasy situation.

As this email seemed more like a favour I offered some of my veterinary experience and suggested that maybe using these injections was hormonally putting this young dog up and down, and he really didn't know what his status was! As for Rufus's over-enthusiastic attention, maybe Tom was emitting female pheromones? I said I thought that balance in their pecking order must be all over the place but, to be honest, I didn't know, but hoped that was of some help. I said the easiest thing would be to ask the dogs themselves, so maybe consider doing that and come back to me if you want to.

The next day a photo arrived through of Rufus, the older one, and I emailed them an appointment. I did my usual spiel at the start, asking if he understood how this worked and then for some reason, unbeknown to me, I asked David what country his accent came from. He replied, "Mmm, I don't know, I am English."

"Oh," I replied, "I thought there was a bit of an exotic accent in there, sorry!" He laughed gently and said, "Oh, it has been said that I talk rather posh, so I suppose it could be that!" Then I realised that the first introduction line I had been given from Rufus, minutes before the call, "I am a true gent, the type that would stand back and say, 'Oh no, you first'!" was said in the same delightful and eloquent way. As soon as I told David this, he laughed and then said, "That is exactly him!"

I did the various chit-chats with Rufus and then got onto the pressing point, Tom. I asked him what he thought of Tom, and he told me that he liked him although he sometimes was very bossy. I pushed further and not once did he show any animosity or fear of him, and then asked me if he was okay? I checked with David and he assured me Tom was okay. "So, why do you ask?" I put to Rufus.

Sounding very worried, he said, "He is… he is ill, he is rather quiet," and this was coupled with a picture of a dog fervently licking another behind its ear.

"That's it!" David exclaimed, "That is exactly what he keeps doing," and then anxiously asked, "Please ask him not to, as that is why Tom bit him last time."

Immediately Rufus defended Tom, "No, he grabbed my leg, like someone would grab your arm to stop you, but just did it a bit hard."

"A bit hard?" repeated David, "he gave him a deep puncture wound, and we had to take him to the vets. We are now too frightened to let them be in the same room together. In fact, last night I slept in the spare room with Rufus!"

Rufus immediately presented me with some of his personal humour by saying, "And he snored!!" I laughed and asked David, in a roundabout way, if he snored, and he quickly confirmed he had been known to!

I went back to this incessant licking and looked carefully at the picture and told David I thought this looked just like what a bitch would do with a puppy to stimulate it to move. I then said I felt this was what Rufus was trying to do. This all made a lot of sense as Tom, having had his hormone suppressant injection again, was now much quieter and the confusion between these dogs was immense. Again I stressed, I am not getting any fear anxiety from Rufus at all, so said I thought that was a positive.

Now we knew the licking was not down to Tom smelling a bit feminine as I had logically thought, I had to now get through to Rufus that Tom was not ill or poorly in any shape or form; He was just quieter than he had been and to stop worrying about him. Rufus understood and suggested that David put some form of oil (I thought it was Eucalyptus he was talking about) behind Tom's ears and a drop on his back, to remind Rufus of this conversation confirming the lack of illness and as a repellent. David said he thought they had some or Oil of Olbas, which we thought would be similar, so I suggested he offer that or Tea Tree, or the like, to Rufus to sniff, and whichever he backed off from, to use that one. I also asked Rufus if he had any other ideas of how to make life easier and he suggested St. John's Wort as that would keep them both quiet! I told David what I heard, and he immediately said, "Oh yeah, we have got some here, it sometimes grows in the garden!" I said I was familiar with its use for nervous dispositions but to please check with a vet about giving it to your dog, unless you really know what you are doing.

We then had a logical conversation about castration as David had said he and Sue had decided they would get Tom 'done'. As soon as he said that, I heard the number twelve. As I do, I ask people if there is any relevance to that number? Maybe the castration was booked for January 12th? "Oh, no," David replied, we have got months in hand as his injection (chemical castration) won't wear off until April.

I said, "Are you not then going to be back in the same boat, why not do it sooner, rather than later? If you leave it until after his injection wears off, it will then be another three months until all his male hormones subside, and he will have to go through another unnecessary hormonal rollercoaster. So, if your vet agrees, and he is done soon, by the time his injection wears off, his male hormones won't be able to return anyway!" David said that sounded sensible to him too.

I wished him, and his wife, a very Merry Christmas and asked that he please let me know the outcome, good or bad.

This is such a difficult situation to be in, but my views on castration were clarified by the stray cat that featured in my first book. He told us (once he was castrated) that life for male non-breeding animals was easier as a 'neutral' as it removes unnecessary testosterone fuelled issues. To live in peace is what most of us desire, and so do most animals too.

Early January an email arrived from David with the update. Fortunately, I always tell people during a reading that I make no promises things will work and just as well - as the oil did not repel Rufus away from Tom at all, although I forgot to ask David how the sniff test went prior to using it. BUT, Rufus *did* take on board that Tom was not ill, and stopped mithering him like an anxious mother. The St. John's Wort certainly did its job too. Peace and a balance had been achieved, and I am sure it would stay that way after the castration which David assured me was imminent.

In his email he also wrote:

'Sue and I would like to thank you very much for your help. Incidentally, I don't know how you talk to our animals but one thing convinces me that you do, and funnily it is because of a mistake. One of the first things you mentioned was a Great Dane with both ears being solid black, which is very unusual for a Harlequin and you thought it might have been Rufus; in fact, this would have been Boston who passed away several years ago and who I never told you anything about him! He had a tremendous personality and sometimes we feel he is still around.'

Now that's what I call validation! Bless them all.

Neither a Leader nor a Follower be

Just because we have been born with legs, does this mean we enjoy jogging? Some people do, they love it, but others, it fills them with dread at the thought of doing it! By now you probably realise I spend my life comparing animals to people, and every day I am shown how similar these characteristics can be.

Take Beau, for example, he was a seven year old, sixteen hand horse and would be described as 'scopey', in other words very athletically built, so full of promise. His owner, Jane, was such a lovely lady to talk to and I felt so sorry for her trying to express how much this horse was struggling to enjoy the things she expected of him. He put this across in his own clear way, "We have been battling for three years, haven't we?" As hard as these words were to hear, Jane agreed and said that is why she had come to me.

The first thing he showed me was a picture of him cantering across open land, which Jane said they did on the odd occasion and she enjoyed that. I said to look on that as a positive as at least he is acknowledging being ridden and looks happy covering the countryside. The problem was the more she tried to teach him the more resistance he put up. When Beau described his time being broken[1] to ride, he said, "It was one step forward, and two steps back, and it is still the same now!" Again, I felt for his owner as she only wanted the best for him and clearly had been extremely patient.

She said, "I absolutely love him, but you are right, it is just a battle and I don't know what to do."

"I'm like my grandsire, he was tricky as well", came the defensive comment from Beau.

Jane gasped and went silent, then said, "Well, you have completely thrown me now, that is exactly what several of my friends have pointed out to me!" It turned out I even knew who his grandsire was and, as with people, sometimes quirks and attitude can be passed on through breeding.

Jane said to ask him about jumping, and he obliged with a quick're-run', and although he jumped well, he looked to be getting more and more hesitant the further he went. She said that was him to a tee and asked why, as he is so capable, does he do this? We had already established that underneath he was not as brave as he was trying to come across and he said, "I would be jumping the first and worrying about the third!!" This was so typical of him but, like a person, if you are a worrier, you are a worrier; it is a hard problem to overcome.

Fortunately, he interspersed his comments with some of the nice things he enjoyed, and one that made me laugh was the fact that Jane made sure his stable was immaculate. The bed made with mathematical precision so it was pleasing to her eye as well as perfect comfort for him. Also, he was a pleasure to handle and reciprocated her affection; and thank goodness for that, otherwise this communication would have been extremely hard work emotionally.

I had now established what kind of horse he was; kind-hearted but with a mind that was being overruled by this undercurrent of fear, courtesy of his breeding. Jane said although she wanted to compete etc., could I please ask him if he still wants to.

His reply could not have been more candid if he had tried, "If your child was scared of getting up on the stage, would you send them to stage school?!" We actually both admired him for his clever use of words and said it made total sense, so what did he want out of life? He simply did not want any pressure and even showed me a picture of himself trying to hide behind another horse.

I asked her if this is what happens when riding in company, and she said, "Yes, and as much as I try to keep him in front, he will find an opportunity to stop, and then land up behind again." I checked if he was quite happy when 'in behind' another horse, and he was. He explained that some people are leaders and some are followers, and he was the latter. I asked why she felt she had to keep making him try to be the lead horse, and she said simply that people say that horses should really do either, shouldn't they?

I pointed out that some people are confident and would happily walk into a room first, but others say, "Okay, you first." Whichever type of person you are, there is not a right or wrong involved here, and I am sure you would find it uncomfortable and maybe rather impertinent should someone insist you go first when in fact it makes no difference who leads through the doorway.

Jane took this all on board, and Beau was very honest by suggesting, "If I am not what she really wants I am sorry, but as I am not vicious or nasty I would suit someone that did not want the pressure of competing either." Oh bless, Jane obviously found this heartfelt offer hard to listen to but said she would now take time to digest all this and keep me informed as to what happens. She thanked me for opening her eyes and giving such a truthful insight into her horse. Also for the realisation that just because they are built to do some form of work they might not necessarily want to, or be mentally strong enough to do it. A couple of days later, Jane emailed me to say she was feeling a lot closer to him and thanked me immensely. She was going to try it his way and see how she felt about giving up on her competitive side, but was feeling positive that now she knew how he ticked, life would be a lot easier.

Beau and Jane's story is an example of my work where it demonstrates that there are some things you cannot change; simply; he was what he was, and at least he got to tell us 'straight from the horse's mouth'. As with anything, if you know what you are dealing with, good or bad, then you at least can make informed decisions to the best of your capability, and that goes for animals as well as people.

[1] An unfortunate description of teaching a horse how to be ridden.

"Horses never leave you; they just become an unseen part of you."
Lovely words given from a horse, to his new owner, knowing he was replacing his mare that had recently died.

"She'd wrap me up in cotton wool if she could, but I'd look very silly!
A horse talking about his ever so loving owner.

"I am every child's dream pony; there is not an ounce of malice in me."
A very true statement from a truly treasured pony that everybody in their pony club would give their 'eye teeth' for.

"I don't mind it too much; I just don't want to do it too much!"
A very fair answer given when asking a horse his views on doing dressage.

Much Ado about Everything

At the end of my first book, I wrote about 'coincidence' or, as I say, 'There is no such thing'. I wrote a biographical poem showing how people are put in the right place, at the right time, to help others, and in this story shows you how this works. Not long after that book had been published, I was taking a trip to visit Rhiannon, a lovely friend of mine, whose dog I had chatted to on several occasions, and now I was going to have a coffee and meet her boyfriend's dog. On the way, I spotted a tack shop (an equestrian supply store), which I had heard of, but never been to myself. I wavered as to whether to stop and go in there and then, to see if they would stock my book, or do it on the way back. I decided on the latter as I really dislike trying to sell anything, so another few hours delay would be fine! Anyway, Rhiannon had said she knew a shop that would take some of my books, so with a bundle of them and some advertising laminates, I drove on.

I arrived at Rhiannon's house, eventually, (some people find left and right confusing and, bless her, she is one!) but it was worth the misdirections. This little dog was such fun and, with her enthusiasms, let me give a good account of what I do because most people naturally tend to be sceptical until they start to hear the facts rolling out. I also enjoyed the personal introduction to her Great Dane who features in a later story in this book, '*Say Cheese*'.

Afterwards, I was heading back towards home and decided to take the plunge and approach this tack shop about my book. I parked neatly (well, as best possible for me) in their car park, picked up six copies of my book and proceeded to the door. I got within ten feet and thought I recognised the person standing just inside the doorway. "Hello," she said as I entered, and it was only a lady whose four horses I had chatted to, and one of hers even featured in the book! After the quick hello, I introduced myself to the owner and did my best to burble my way through explaining why I thought people would want to buy my book, therefore would they like to stock it? I said I had an advertising laminate also but, after looking in the box, I realised I had left it back at Rhiannon's house so I said I would go out and phone my friend and would be back in a minute. I got it sorted and Rhiannon said she would 'nip' over with it and by the time I got back in the shop, my client must have said something about what I had done for her horses as they agreed to sell the books there and then! A girl was also standing there, who apparently worked there, and it was mentioned that maybe I should talk to her horse, but in a joking way, so I didn't pay much attention. I said my goodbyes and asked if they could let me know if they wanted more.

Within a week, I got a call from Carolyn (the girl in the shop) who said she had read my book and had actually known Julie Dicker, who I had mentioned in it. Julie was a wonderful animal communicator who sadly died in 2006 but had lived in the same area of Exeter as Carolyn. I told her that I had sent a signed copy to Julie's husband, Phil, as I had spoken to him to ask permission to mention her, and he said he would be delighted and would love a signed copy. Carolyn asked me if I could chat to her horse, Othello, and I said I would be happy to and said I would email her about all the relevant details required. That same evening, the client that I had met at the tack shop phoned about a dental problem with her young horse, and I mentioned that Carolyn had booked in and she said, "Oh, that's good, she thinks he might have Cushing's disease!" (This tends to be an older horse/pony disease, sometimes linked to the pituitary gland but just to be difficult there is also a type that isn't). I stopped her quickly and asked her not to tell me any more.

Othello turned out to be a 20-year-old black (I know technically I should say dark brown, but to me some horses are black, so that is what I write) with Hackney in his breeding. He was very stunning, and boy, didn't he know it! As usual I asked him to tell me something about himself, he declared, "I am such a straight mover!" and then, very sweetly, "but I am a bit of a baby when it comes to pain!!" I repeated this to Carolyn and she recognised them both, so, as I had now validated I was talking to him, I said I would let him chat away and see what came up. I did, however, inform her that my client had told me about her medical suspicions, just in case she thought I was 'cheating' or such like. With that, Othello butted in saying, "I don't think things are half as bad as she thinks they are"

I don't diagnose, but carefully repeated his opinion, and she said, 'Good!' As we were on the medical side of things, he decided we should pursue that route, so gave me the most uncomfortable feeling in my buttocks, and the strange feeling as if I wanted to dip my back, as if to lift what would be his quarters. He also gave me a picture of what looked like fatty lumps, so now I had a mixture of things to discuss, but nothing about the 'Cushing's disease'. Carolyn understood the pictures and said that is how he stands, as if holding his backside higher than it should be! As for the fatty lumps, well, Othello had got rather overweight and was now on a diet.

Carolyn said since they had moved, he had got a problem with the grass, to which he neatly replied, "No, *she* has the problem with the grass!" Ah, this pony was not impressed with the diet, but again Carolyn was concerned that he had grown this fat crest on his neck and although he lost weight, it had not really gone down much. This was on her list of symptoms that she had got from the internet that she thought were all relative to Cushing's disease. Othello thought this was quite amusing so decided to put himself in the 'doctor's chair', but giving himself the questions, and answering them too!!

"Am I still eating normally? ...Yes!"

Carolyn's reply, "Err, yes!"

"Am I tired and falling asleep all the time … No!"

But as Carolyn said, a difficult one to answer as she is not with him all day, but he didn't seem tired, so we agreed with his 'No'.

"Am I acting like a sick horse? ... No!"

She agreed.

"Am I weeing more than usual?… No!"

Carolyn agreed again and, by this time, I wasn't thinking he was very ill and she was thinking he had read her symptoms list!

He also said he thought he was changing his coat (a typical sign of Cushing's is when they don't shed it and it gets long and curly) and he did have a lovely summer coat. Unfortunately he is always fully clipped out as soon as his winter coat arrives, so it is quite hard to tell if it would have been a long/curly coat had it been left as nature intended.

He enhanced the feeling of discomfort and showed me someone treating his back, flicking down the vertebrae as they do, coupled with a sarcastic, "If you must," comment from Othello. This corresponded to his initial declaration of being a baby where pain was concerned. He then proceeded to show me a picture of him really showing off, pushing his quarters under him, then saying, "Sometimes that is my downfall." This horse, well actually I had presumed he was a horse, but in fact he is, by height, only a pony, but very well known as he competes at medium dressage against all the big horses, and wins!! In his eyes, he is a horse, so I shall call him one too. Although Carolyn had had his back treated several times over the past eighteen months, things were still not as they should be but he still worked when asked to, however, generally was not as he used to be. I asked him if he knew what had happened. He simply replied, "I fell on my arse," and after a piece of fast judgement, I repeated it!

Carolyn took me aback by saying, "He wouldn't say that!"

And Othello replied, "I don't think arse is a bad word, do you?" Well, we both cracked up, and to be honest this lad was so 'gung ho' that a word like that I would not have thought as offensive. (On very rare occasions animals have sworn but their language is, on the whole, far nicer than most of what we hear today.) So back to his fall, he showed me him careering round the field, trying to skid to a halt before the fence line but his backside carried on and, in a split second, he was on his…bottom! However, as funny as this sounds, actually it was not. You know that horrible trick some children used to play at school when they pulled your seat from under you just as you went to sit down? Well this had the same effect but in a much bigger body. The impact had ricocheted up his spine and he felt whiplashed through his back, straining many of his muscles with it. This made complete sense as she had not had a fall on him, so to have such muscle problems, which she was aware of, could be the key to the puzzle.

He then 'shot' me a horrible taste of saltiness in my mouth, and told me to tell her that he knew when she was putting 'extra stuff' in his feed. Carolyn gasped and said she had just started putting salt in his food as it had been recommended somewhere that this was important if a horse sweats. He asked for a bit less and said that he thought a potassium-related one would be better. Neither she nor I knew what he meant, so I suggested we should look it up on the internet. And, guess what? I have just looked it up as I write this story and the answer - potassium chloride is another kind of salt!!" I learn something new every day, and today this was it.

I asked him what he thought would help him, now for a horse that doesn't like pain, this answer was a surprise - acupuncture! This, to me, seemed logical as he had a lack of energy flow through his muscles as this was a deep-seated problem. I knew of a vet who, according to many, was very good, so Carolyn said she would be happy to travel him there for treatment.

I wished her the best of luck and asked her to keep me up-to date on his progress. I have to say, it was such a lovely communication to do, we just laughed and laughed, and he was kind enough to show me a picture from long ago of Julie with him and Carolyn. He showed me that Julie was a gentle lady with a quiet manner; quite the opposite of me, when I get funny horses like this I treat it like a chat with a comedian and enjoy it for all it's worth! It's the animal's frame of mind that gives me my feelings, so if something is sad, then so am I, but as the saying goes, 'smile, and the world smiles with you'.

We finished the call, with both our sides aching for sure, but just before we went, she said, "Can you ask him about our special day?"

So I did, and with that, the cheeky boy said, "Oh, *we* didn't get married you know!"

I laughed and repeated the bizarre response, and Carolyn said, "No, but I did, and I rode him to the church!!" Oh bless, could you imagine this stunning black horse, decked out with beautiful ribbons and a stunning bride to match? Those wedding photos would be well worth a look!

After Christmas, Carolyn phoned me to thank me for doing a very special communication for a friend of hers, which, incidentally, has encouraged me to ask for spirit animals when it is right, but that is a whole story in itself. In one of my future books I will write their story which, I promise you, will prove to you that they simply 'move' to heaven and carry on living. Carolyn took the opportunity to tell me about Othello and her update on him too. He had been to the vets for his acupuncture and the vet sided with Othello saying that she didn't think he had Cushing's disease either! She recognised his muscle problem and in her opinion this was actually being exacerbated by slight liver and kidney function problems, which, unfortunately, older animals can suffer from, as can people. So after falling on his 'backside' and as much as the muscles were trying to repair, if the body is not functioning as it should, sadly, their fibres can't heal and become relaxed muscle as the body would wish it to be. He had his acupuncture which Carolyn found fascinating as, although it sounds quite technical, the vet was using it to stimulate his body. So, if his body functions worked better, then they would help remove the toxins from his body quicker, so the muscles would be less affected. Carolyn also bought him a liver tonic, which I have also heard has great effect at helping getting their systems cleared. The other thing that tickled me was that Carolyn went through Othello's medical information she had gathered over the years and, at one point, he had been potassium deficient, so no wonder he was trying to guide us on the type of salt!

I am sure he will continue to improve, and I hope they continue to have fun and enjoy each other. I only found out when I spoke to her about writing this that Carolyn used to be a PE (physical exercise) instructor but had an operation on her feet that had gone wrong. This stopped her running so someone suggested she got a horse! She had never even ridden a horse, yet owned one, and look where they have got to today! They have won many competitions, but the main thing - Othello put the smile back on her face, and if anybody could make you feel good, Othello certainly would.

So, I hope you can see what happened here. My time was delayed going into the tack shop so then my client was 'in place' to speak up for my work, and let my books spread the word. I had left the laminate behind which gave an opportunity for a quick discussion to take place out of my presence. Carolyn worked in the tack shop and needed help with the gorgeous Othello and it was Carolyn's friend whose dogs, Phoebe and Connie, had both tragically died young. I was then called upon to ask to speak to them in heaven. They both spoke to me and this helped the lady and brought such peace to her, but also it gave me the push to offer to do this for others. If they were just a 'set of coincidences' - well, they were great ones! I will leave you to decide, but once you start to see the synchronicity, you will, I think, come to the same conclusion: these are not 'coincidences', they are simply organised 'connections'.

Unexpected

We have known Ann, a dental client, for many years and were surprised when she phoned and asked me for help. She is lovely and I would describe her as very traditional in her ways so was quite taken aback when she said, "I had heard from Sarah of the work you do, and I know this sounds strange but I fell off my horse and as it happened so quickly, neither my friend nor I know what happened. Is there any possibility you could ask him?"

"Okay," I agreed but said that I would treat him like any other case, have a chat to get to 'know' him and then I would see what I could find out. I did however point out that one, he might not want to talk about it, and two, he maybe wouldn't remember, but I could ask and see how it goes.

Max was a grey Connemara cross, about twelve years old and was very chatty and quite 'a card!' Ann had only owned him for a few years and, although she recognised most of the things he told us, there was one thing that she didn't really recollect so she didn't know if it was true or not. The subject in question was the delight he took in moving anything about in the stable that you happen to forget to take with you! He was very gentle, sometimes a bit physically sensitive with his girth and such like, but a very good and loving horse who enjoyed his hunting and fun rides.

I asked him if he could show us anything that could help recollect what had happened about a week previously when Ann had 'come to grief'. He instantly gave me a picture of a left bend with obvious foot skids scored across the soft ground, and a matching pair to be precise. "Oh my goodness, that's exactly what Sarah saw when she caught him and led him back, so it looks like his feet had gone from under him, doesn't it?" I agreed and checked with Max, who showed me him losing his balance and falling to his left side, but fortunately, Ann had fallen away from him. She and her pride were only gently bruised but she was pleased to have the mystery cleared up and that it was an accident, nothing intentional. Bob was due to do Max's teeth soon so I said I would try to come out with him too.

About a month later we were on her yard doing the lovely Max's teeth and Ann was quick to inform me that she had spoken to his previous owner and casually asked if she had ever noticed him moving things that were left in his stable? Apparently this was true - he'd been a monkey for knocking things off; whatever they left on a ledge, he would push it off, be it cream, hoof picks, dandy brushes or even a coffee mug, so they learnt very quickly not to do it! Whilst I was there she asked me if I could have a quick word with him and ask if there was anything she could do to help his great discomfort about his girth being tightened. He was not nasty in any way, but went so tense that Ann had to do his girth up very slowly and carefully. She had to get on him as if he were an egg that might break, but after a minute or so, he would relax and all would be fine. Max pointed out that there was a very deep muscle that was somehow connected through the underside length of him and, as the girth was tightened, it gave him a horrible pulling sensation deep into his stomach area. I had to admit I really didn't know what he was talking about, but likened it to an elastic band, so if you pulled it up at one part that maybe it went taut in another?! I asked Max what treatment he thought would help and he said something that would make this muscle more relaxed so that it could stretch easier. Ann knew a physio who used lasers for deep muscle problems so said she would get in touch with her. With the dental over, we left and I asked her to let me know if a muscle like this does exist, as the more physical information I learn the more it helps me understand what I am shown.

Ann kept her word and informed me that there was such a muscle and the physio had found that he had a problem there, and after two treatments he was much better, not perfect, but much better.

Bob came back from work one day and said, "Ann is in hospital, apparently she has a broken leg!" I quickly phoned my friend who confirmed this and said Ann had been out hunting and had a really bad fall, been knocked unconscious and it was an 'air ambulance job'. I asked her to keep me up-to-date on how Ann was getting on, and she also assured me that Max was perfectly fine. (I do appreciate at this point that some of you reading this might be anti-hunt, but I stay impartial whether it is hunting, Parelli, polo etc. as my work is to help the animals. If those animals go hunting then I feel I must do what I can to help them be as comfortable and happy doing it.)

A month passed and Ann had left hospital and it was like a repeat performance trying to find out once again what had happened. I tuned in with Max and he said he was fine but felt abandoned as he had not seen Ann. This upset her but she explained that she could still barely walk and could not get down the field to see him, so I told him that she would as soon as she physically could. He was desperately sad that she had been hurt and showed me 'clear as day' what had happened; they had been going across a very steep field and riding across the camber when Ann and a group had stopped and waited for others. As Ann set off to the left, his backend slipped out to the right, causing him to 'fold' in the middle. This then shunted his saddle forward making him panic and, as he spun round, he threw Ann off like a rag doll down the bank. This happened in seconds and he ran off absolutely terrified, but was fortunately caught by someone and eventually taken home. Ann said it made total sense as she remembered exactly where they were at the time and that did sound feasible. She thanked me and asked me if she could come back to me when she was fit to ride again as she was now very worried that she had lost her nerve with him, as this was the second fall off him within a year, and she could count the previous falls she had had in the past thirty years on one hand! I, of course, said it was 'no problem' and that I felt that Max was rather unnerved by the whole experience also.

Time passed and again Ann phoned. She really was struggling and as much as she loved him, she had decided she would sell him. She admitted that she was fine riding around the roads but, although he never put a foot wrong, as soon as he set foot on grass she tensed so badly that she just couldn't bring herself to do it. Could I please explain that she is selling him because she loves him and wants him to go to a good home. He would then get to do more hunting and jumping which he adores and does with relish, rather than stand in her field doing nothing for the rest of his days. He was a complete gent about the whole thing, said he quite understood. He assured her all would be well and for her not to feel guilty about the situation, it was just one of those things.

Ann put the word out, and within a month Max had been sold to a lovely family that lived not that far away. He had passed the vet; they had collected him and said they would let her know how he was going. Well, they were delighted with him, he was being an absolute star, they were treating him with the love and sensitivity he deserved and they were over the moon with him.

Ann left it a few months then put out the word that she was now looking for a new horse, about the same size as Max, fifteen hands, or maybe even a bit smaller. She had been to see a couple but no joy, but when having a conversation saying what she wanted, two friends said 'Josh' at the same time. Ann thought if the two of them thought he would be worth looking at, and then maybe she should too. She phoned the owner who informed her that he wasn't in fact for sale, but, she could have him on permanent loan as he had failed a sale vetting due to a slight leg problem. Undeterred she set off to see if Josh was the one for her. Well, she about fainted when she saw him, he was at least sixteen hands plus, really not what she had expected! But, she was there so if he truly was 'Mr Safe' then she would try him. He was a total dream to ride; he just wandered along when she wanted and sped up only when she asked. Much to her and her husband's surprise, she said she would love to have him. Soon he was collected and settled in just like he had lived there all his life. A true test was given to him in the first week when the floods occurred and he walked through swirling water about two feet deep to get in from his paddock to the yard, without a moment's hesitation or silliness.

I had the delight in meeting this lovely lad who happily chatted away and said that he liked the fact this was a personal home, as he had actually lived on a big yard. He said, "I am quite forward going you know!"

Ann looked at me quizzically and said, "I don't know about that, I have to keep asking him to go along when I am exercising him!"

"Oh," I replied, rather confused, "Well, maybe he thinks that is forward going?!"

Ann then asked me to ask him about hunting, and he said, "I think I will get a bit excited but not stupid." I wished them both well and hoped he was true to his word. The next time I spoke to her she said she had now hunted him, and yes, he did get excited, was rather forward going but not stupid and had looked after her. She smiled and said she was getting braver by the week!

This was a situation that Ann never expected to be in, and would dearly have loved to have kept Max, but sometimes if you lose your nerve on one horse you can still be fine on another, and this was the case. So through communication we were able to establish the truth about both falls: there was no ill intent, so she was able to sell him as the honest horse she always thought he was. And, as for the new boy; he was not up to being a competition horse any more but was still perfectly able to be a hunting/fun horse and I am sure will be most content with that.

One question I had to ask Ann, as I am sure quite of few of you horse owners are thinking… "If you have the intention of buying a small horse, or even an 'up to height' pony, what would make you change your mind and not worry about the height difference?"

And this was her answer: "The only reason I was contemplating buying a smaller version was because I am not as young as I used to be and do struggle to get on from the ground. So, I thought a smaller one would solve that problem, but it didn't make any difference as I found my 'spring' had gone, and still had to find a bank to stand on or clamber up a gate to mount from. Josh had stood stock-still at every gate for me to get on him, so under these circumstances I thought what difference would going one bar higher on the gate make?!" I agreed with her, you couldn't argue with that!!

Trapped

Some readings are just an absolute pleasure to do, and when I received a picture of a magnificent black Friesian horse, it turned into one of those very special and personal conversations. The horse had been bought for the lady by her father who, sadly, had passed over earlier that year. This stunning horse had no problems or issues really, she just wanted to hear what he had to say and his whole conversation was bliss. What made it so special was his comment, "He can still grow flowers in Heaven, you know," which I quickly turned round in my head and gently asked if her father had enjoyed gardening.

"Oh, yes," she replied, "he adored his garden." I then gave her the words as her horse had spoken, which although brought tears, they were tears of joy with a true understanding that her father was still around, and his wonderful last gift was proving that.

Thanks to the above reading this led on to me trying to help a lady with her fairly newly acquired coloured horse. Beth, his owner, had phoned me and asked how she could go about getting a communication done as she was not on the internet I gave her my address and she said she would post the photo to me. The letter arrived within a couple of days and I was slightly confused as there were two photos inside, but of two different horses! I read the letter and realised why she had put in the extra photo of her 'old boy', that looked very well, and the lad I was to talk to, that looked very thin by comparison. I am guessing that she was worried that had she just sent me the picture of a poor-looking horse, I might have been led to think this was maybe down to her standard of care, so sensibly she used her retired old boy as proof of her knowledge of good horse management.

This youngster was rising four years old, called Bentley, and was black and white with a lot of feathers (hair) round his feet, and was just about over the pony height. Coloured cobs are renowned for being kind, gentle, and tolerant and good-doers (could live on 'fresh air' as is often said). When Beth went to see him, she could see his gentle eye but he was scrawny, nervy and not the laid-back horse you would expect for his type. It was, sadly, a typical 'rough' dealing yard, but fortunately, Beth could see past the angst and knew she had to buy him as she felt desperately sorry for this poor young animal. She had him vetted and although it was noted that he was very underweight, he was physically sound, and although it had turned into a bit of a trial when her vet was trying to feel his limbs she was undeterred and bought him.

Beth gave him a couple of months to settle in (and to put on weight), then had gently taught him the basics and had begun to ride him. Sadly, things were going from bad to worse so she decided to get me involved to see exactly what was going on.

As soon as I talked to him, he was like a quivering child, trying not to go wrong, but not being able to help himself. He gave me the feeling of being girthed, like he would freeze: "If I don't move maybe nothing will happen." Beth said that is him all over, he does this 'frightened rabbit' impression. I asked him to show me him being ridden. He showed me the mounting block with him frozen to the spot and even when Beth sat in the saddle but as soon as he was asked to go forward, he shot off. This she recognised and said that he keeps doing it and even when ridden, he stops and starts and then shoots off and, to be honest, it was getting dangerous. I asked him to show me and try to explain what he was feeling. He constantly gave me the feeling of 'being chased' from behind, then a picture of a pony-trap.

"Has this pony been driven?" I enquired, and she said that it could well be possible but could not be sure. I said that, by the pictures, I felt he was trying to tell me he had and that was what he felt was chasing him. With that, he gave me the feeling of being weak and trying to hold the weight and pressure of a trap behind him when going downhill. He also kept showing me his feet looking rough and 'raggedy' and implied they were sore. Again, this was a bit vague as Beth said he was not lame and on his vetting he was definitely not lame. I said we would just acknowledge this and move on.

I set about trying to see what I could do to 'undo' his fears and as, fortunately, Beth had no intention of driving him I could assure him that a cart would not be put behind him. He said, "I am a bit of a confused young man." I asked him to expand on that, and he said that although he knew Beth was not trying to hurt him, he just could not override that fear. I asked to start with the fear about being girthed, and he immediately threw me the horrible picture of him being roped down and being castrated, with no anaesthetic or pain relief. That thought might fill you with horror, but sadly, although I hope rarely, it does go on. So now you can imagine how an animal feels when you try to put another type of restrictive item on it, it can bring back horrendous memories, as it was doing with Bentley. I explained that the people that did that were ignorant, cruel beyond belief, but nothing like that would ever happen to him again. I asked him to give me words for Beth to use when she was trying to touch his body, and he gave me, "I'm just checking, not hurting." And, to help when tacking him up, he asked her to say, "It's just for fun, I promise." So Beth noted that down and said she would use them. On to the riding and I asked him to tell me why he would do this 'stop and start, then rush off' thing. He cried, "I'm not stupid, I only wanted to look, but as soon as I looked, they beat me."

He recalled, "Stupid horse, get on, get on, you stupid thing!" which was what some person riding him had said every time he slowed to 'take in' an unfamiliar object. I know we all make mistakes and sometimes can say mean things to people let alone our animals, but the odd ones would be quickly forgiven and forgotten; however, this was a daily occurrence for this young horse, and this is what he thought what 'to be ridden' was all about. I explained all this to Beth and she said she realised how 'unworldly-wise' he was and would treat him like a complete baby again if that helped. He thought that sounded good, and asked if he was to pause at something, could she please let him and tell him he was 'clever'. This we thought was very apt and told him we thought he was very clever to think of that as a word to say, as it is a very clever thing to do, to look and learn. We covered the issue of him rushing off and the dangers if he got out of control, for himself let alone Beth.

I felt this was a very genuine little horse, I even wrote on my records, genuine+++, so I thanked him for trusting me enough to talk to him and wished them both well.

As it turned out, both Beth's and my feelings were proven to be right! This little horse, actually, not so little now, has grown and is now a full up-to-weight, well-muscled horse and, in fact, barely recognisable. Beth followed his requests and he has come on in leaps and bounds. He is so relaxed; she can groom him, tack him up and ride him with no signs of fear whatsoever. The feeling of being chased by a trap is a distant memory and he got to pause and learn, and now he goes past anything and everything. He is having a well-earned rest over this frozen winter of 2009/10, which has put paid to most forms of work let alone sport! As I said, Beth doesn't have email (and is taking great joy in trying to be the last person to be converted!) so refreshingly, I had the update via phone call.

It was so wonderful to hear how they were both doing and the sheer joy that this had brought them both and I am so glad to have been a part of it. Beth said that she had found out some things since our conversation. Apparently, when she was on Bentley's previous yard she had noticed another horse and asked about it and had been told it was on box rest as it had damaged its legs. She had found out since that the horse in question had got injured as it bolted from its field at the sight of a pony and empty trap careering flat out up their rough pot-holed road! So Bentley's trap issue was confirmed and probably the reason for his mention of his sore feet too.

She told me that recently she had to call the vet out to Bentley as he somehow had managed to stake himself underneath up into the groin area – sounds worse than it was! He was a great patient for Beth as she had bathed it and put cream on it but it looked like there was a pocket of infection, so hence the vet call.

The vet turned up and he was the same one that had done Bentley's vetting six months earlier and, going on previous experience of this horse, entered cautiously ready for 'battle to ensue' but to an abrupt halt as Bentley pricked his ears and stood there quite contented! Beth told me the vet just leant against the wall and said, "Gosh, he is like a different horse, and not just in the physical sense but mentally too!" Beth said that he was a changed animal and, sure enough, he was. He let the vet work under in the area that had originally left him with such horrendous memories. Bentley didn't flinch or worry; just stood with Beth at his head, knowing that no harm would ever come to him. With his treatment completed, she said the vet was still shaking his head in disbelief and said he was so pleased for her, and left with the biggest smile on his face!

If one horse deserved such a good owner, it was certainly Bentley. Beth says this summer they will be going on bed and breakfast holidays where they will ride from place to place, across beautiful hills and countryside, and I am sure if Bentley pauses to take in the views that Beth will be wanting to do the same.

Up the Shoot

As I was passing the local odds and ends/second hand shop, I said 'Hi' to the shop dog as usual. He was a Labrador cross, with a large dash of white down the centre of his head, earning him the name Badger. I had previously had an hilarious chat with him, as he has seen many things come and go in life, which would go with the territory of this type of shop; although full of little treasures, I'm sure, but it was navigating your way through the less desirable items that was certainly a challenge. I had a lot of time for the owner, Neil, as back when I was bald from my cancer, but dressed in some bright coloured bandana, he would often comment that I still had a smile on my face whatever, and would wish me luck. So, on this day, I was some way past his shop when he appeared, as if in a puff of smoke, and breathlessly said that a lady, Michaela, had a cat that desperately needed my help. He asked me to come back as he would get his mobile and give her a call, if okay with me. A bit confused and bemused, I agreed to listen to the call. He told her that he had tracked me down and had me in the shop, and she could talk to me now! I sensed her urgency but said the easiest thing for me to do was to take her number and I promised to phone her when I got home.

Immediately I got back to my house, I grabbed a cuppa and sat down to give this lady, Michaela, a call. She answered the phone straight away as if she had been sitting on it! She quickly explained that she knew I was the person to help her as she did Reiki and believed in alternative treatments. As nobody could figure out what was going on with Stanley, could I come and ask him? Stanley was a beautiful Chocolate Point Siamese, with dark tips on his ears, feet and the end of his tail. She asked me if I could come as soon as possible as he really was getting more poorly by the day. I rarely visit animals, as most of my work is done 'at a distance' but as he was only two miles away it made sense and seemed a quicker way than to wait for her to send me a photograph.

I pulled into a sweeping drive near a church and could see various cats through the window. I was directed past a small menagerie by Michaela and into the kitchen to be met personally by Stanley himself. Michaela made sure all doors were shut as these were house cats and, due to the fast road below, it would have been foolhardy to let them out. Sat on the counter, like a china ornament, was Stanley. He was still a stunning cat, even with his obvious lack of weight, combined with a somewhat dull, lacklustre coat. He was sitting quietly surveying me as I quickly explained to Michaela how I worked and that whatever he told me I would pass on and see what we could find out.

As usual, I don't just 'zoom' in questions about an illness, which, incidentally, had been going on for months. Although she was sure her Reiki was really helping him, she needed to know more as the vets were rather at a loss as to what was wrong with him. He chatted away, as they do; he was such a sensitive and loving boy, so gentle and thoughtful, and was so sad for her, as she was for him. He shared with me the nauseous feelings and repeated pictures of eating then throwing it all back up within a short space of time, so I decided to ask him then if he had any idea what was wrong with him. He gave me a very bizarre picture which I got him to repeat, just to be sure. I conveyed it to Michaela, saying I really didn't think it made sense but it looked like he was chewing a light coloured, wood-type tree!! And to make things seem even odder, he showed me a long slim-pointed slither which also seemed to be of wood! To my amazement, she jumped up and said, "I understand exactly what you are talking about, I have seen him do it and it's the bamboo tree."

"But I thought they didn't go out?" I replied.

"Oh, they don't, we have one in the house and I have seen him chewing at it."

"I didn't think a cat would chew a tree but, anyway, what is with the little shards of wood, he doesn't chew it that hard surely?"

"They are the bamboo seeds; they are quite long and very sharp."

With that, I immediately was given a very clear picture of this seed-like object, on an angle at the bottom of his gullet, near the entrance of his stomach. By this time, Michaela was quite beside herself, she said she had felt all along that it had been high up and not in the gut area that the vets thought more likely. The vets had said that if they didn't do an exploratory operation on him he would surely die as he was getting weaker by the day, due to the vomiting.

So, armed with my input, she set off to the vets the next day and asked that when they opened him up, could they please look at the entrance to his stomach area to see if he had any damage or a foreign object lodged. Later that day, he was anaesthetised and, to the vet's horror, he found his body cavity was filled with pus. In ninety nine percent of cases, the organs would have been bright red with inflammation and poison, so normally fatal. He duly cleaned him out with a saline solution and, to the vet's amazement, his organs were actually of a semi-normal pink colour and his intestines were not 'glued' together. The area at the entrance of the stomach had a small tear/opening in it, so although the tiny offending object was nowhere to be seen, it had basically cut like a razor and caused food to leak into his body cavity. With his operation over and now back in a kennel attached to a drip, the vet phoned Michaela to give her the news, but with an extremely guarded prognosis. The vet repeated his astonishment at the lack of adhesion of Stanley's intestines and agreed that the constant Reiki healing that she had been giving him must have had a real positive effect.

By late afternoon Stanley had eaten and got past the half hour without being sick. He was fed little by little every few hours and nothing came back up! He wasn't 'out of the woods' but he really was fighting his corner. Within a week, he was a changed boy; he had put on weight and instead of doing that 'pitying whinge', he had regained full vocal strength.

In-between times, I had moved house so did not hear whether he had pulled through or what had been found. As you can imagine, I could not phone and ask her as the worst might have occurred but, once again, Badger's owner appeared in the street, so I took the opportunity to ask him. He told me the cat was fine, back to normal and was sure that Michaela would love to see me as she had been back to thank him for putting me in touch with her.

I drove up that familiar drive and could see and hear Stanley as soon as I approached the door. Stanley was straight up and rubbing himself round my legs and talking away in true Siamese style. He looked so well and was still having Reiki just to be sure! It gave me such pleasure to see him again and, apparently, the bamboo tree had been banished to the garden forever!

Bird Brained!

The majority of people start the New Year with a headache having over-indulged the night before, but me, no, I felt fine and landed up talking to two budgies! You just couldn't make this up!

I had phoned my friend, Helen, to wish her, and her family, a very Happy New Year and all the best for 2010. Helen's ponies featured in my *Animal Insight* book, and their story was a mixture of sadness and some lovely results, this being coupled with how we were 'introduced' thanks to her mother, who had passed to spirit the year before. That sounds strange you may think, but her mother was a clairvoyant/medium and it was no coincidence that we were brought together. Helen has two children, Sam, aged seven, and Hattie, aged five. It was through her husband, Phil, that my book actually landed in the hands of one of the very well-known actors from *Coronation Street,* as one of the actresses is married to one of Phil's friends.. I have to admit Phil was up there amongst the sceptics but has been gracious enough to listen and see the evidence and also the changes that have occurred allowing him to make his own judgement.

I met Helen's children for the first time just before Christmas and we showed Sam, who is obsessed with birds, the picture on my website of me holding a bird of prey. Much to my amazement he exclaimed, "That's a Harris Hawk!!" and blow me, at only seven years old, he was right! Helen said that he was mad about birds but had been told that he would have to wait until he was ten before he could have his own birds although she was only pretending, but they would have to be of a smaller variety. She said that she thought a budgie would be a good idea, but had impressed upon him that he would need to learn all about them and their needs. He found a book from the library and in a week was able to quote it chapter and verse, and apparently, it's unfair to keep just one budgie as they get very lonely and he did not want to make a bird sad.

With Sam none the wiser, Helen managed to track down a breeder and ordered a pair of boys that would be the right age to be collected at Christmas time. She bought the biggest birdcage suitable for them and all the toys and cuttle fish to go with it too. Talk about a 'kid at Christmas', Helen was so excited and Sam truly had no idea whatsoever.

Christmas Eve, 2009, and Sam's dreams came true! Phil brought the children home and there, in all its splendour, was a big shiny cage, complete with two little budgies inside.. Sam was speechless, ran over to introduce himself and promised to look after them, just as his books had told him how. All went smoothly for a couple of days but then they started screeching and squawking whenever they saw, or even seemed to hear, the dog's nails 'clicking' across the laminate floor. A week of this and it had begun to grate on everyone's nerves, and also Helen was frightened they would injure themselves as they were flying about so frantically.

After the initial 'Happy New Year' greetings, Helen laughed as she said, "I need your help again!"

"But you are laughing," I said, relieved it was not something serious.

"I know you have talked to big birds, any chance you could talk to our budgies?"

I just burst out laughing as I hadn't expected this as, firstly, they are budgies and, secondly, I could not imagine what could be wrong. She said that something was seriously upsetting them and she knew she shouldn't tell me more, and with that, I said, "Err, is the dog scaring them?"

"Oh, you're too quick; you have worked it out already. Can I send you a picture?"

"Oh go on, and I will phone you when it comes through, although I don't know if it will be of any help, as how we will identify who we are talking to will be hard, but never mind, take one and send it." My mobile beeped acknowledging a message from Helen. I attached it to my computer and printed up this vague picture of two birds sitting side by side in their cage.

I phoned back asking, "So what do we call Peter and Paul then?" which was my attempt at having a quick recollection of the nursery rhyme, 'Two little birds sitting on a wall...'

Helen replied with, "Steve and Alan!"

"What?" I chortled. "You can't call budgies Steve and Alan!"

"Sam called them that, have you not seen that video on Youtube?!"

"No, why, what is it about?"

"Oh, you need to watch it," she laughed, and then explained that it was Sam's favourite clip as someone had done a funny voice over of a meerkat calling, 'Steve, Steve, Steve', then decided it was Alan he was maybe looking at, so shouts, 'Alan, Alan…', I said I would look it up later.

So, "Which bird is which?" I asked. "Steve is the green one."

"Slight problem, Helen, the whole photo is a blur of green! So let's go for left and right."

"It's Alan on the right."

"Right, I will ask for Alan then!" I kept 'cracking up' as this was just so bizarre and funny.

I did my best to tune in with Alan and was given a picture of Helen's garden shed, which I recognised as I had seen it when I visited, but as they had been threatened to be banished to it, then maybe it was relevant! Helen said they could not see it from where they were so I asked him to tell me something else. I was given a picture of a slightly bent middle toe on a bird's foot! I asked if one of them had a toe bent off to the left and she said that she didn't know but Sam and she would go and look.

"It does!" she exclaimed.

"I think it is on his left foot, yes?" I volunteered.

"Yes, it is," she replied.

"Well, at least I know that I am talking to Alan not Steve," which still sounded absurd apart from the fact they were young budgies with the most bizarre names. "Damn," I said, "why is Phil not there? He could not dispute that evidence of this being genuine!!"

Still laughing, Helen said, "Do you mind if I put you on loudspeaker as Sam wants to listen too?" I said that was fine by me.

I set about trying to get on to the subject of the 'scary dog', which is actually a lovely spaniel called Poppy who is twelve years old. I got a picture of a large metal stand, angled at the top, so asked if that was what their cage was hung on. It wasn't, their cage was actually on a sideboard so unsure of what that was, I dismissed that and carried on. Then Helen said, "Ah, wait a minute, that is our coat stand and they can see it from where they are." With that, I was shown a picture of Poppy (incidentally, the budgies insisted on calling her Polly, which I thought was funny) sitting below it. "Oh, she does", said Helen, "if I am working in that room, she will sit and wait there until I have finished."

"What do you think she is trying to do?" I asked Alan.

"She wants to eat us, she does, she does!" and he gave me the feeling of being flustered, so I set about assuring them she didn't. They showed me her staring up at their cage, and with a real fixed gaze, but what they didn't realise was that she is nearly blind. I tuned into Poppy, whom I have spoken to before, and she assured me she meant no harm and knew what they were, but just wondered 'where were they?' I explained where they were and she asked if I could tell them that she was just curious.

I told them and they wanted Helen to reassure them by saying, "She doesn't want to eat you!" So they now knew that, and Poppy, the dog, now knew exactly where they were, so I left it at that.

Helen asked Sam if he had a question for Alan who, by this time, had declared he was the bossiest bird anyway! Sam wanted to ask when their birthday was!! Difficult one, I find animals can be inaccurate with ages but asked Alan when they thought they were born, and was instantly told, 'End of September'. With a quick bit of finger counting, that made three months, which would be as the breeder had said! Sam asked what day in September, and I said I didn't know that but could he choose September the 25th, as that was my Dad's birthday? Delighted with that, Sam trotted off to put it on the calendar. I asked Alan if he had anything he wanted to say to Sam, and he imitated Sam by saying, "Have the birds got food, Mummy?" and Helen confirmed that he is being very vigilant, just as the books say. Alan then volunteered that Sam was a very special little boy as he told lots of people that he loved them! Ah, how sweet, I thought, and Helen said that he does, he is a very affectionate child. Alan was in his 'budgie-stride' by now and told me that Sam was a very good writer and that he is very careful when he writes, and even showed me his letters which were very rounded to look at. True, and again Helen explained that this would have been seen as he sits near them when he is doing his writing. This made me smile - Helen told me that I am Sam's 'hero' as he had also written a book but as I had got mine published this gave me 'hero' status! Sam had wandered off by then and we finished the call with Helen saying that she would do all the explaining and see what happened.

Phil arrived home later to... gentle tweeting... "What have you done to the budgies?" he questioned.

"Err, mmm, err, I got Jackie to talk to them!!!"

Phil shook his head laughingly and said, "No, I can't believe you got Jackie to talk to them!"

"But it has worked hasn't it? Try walking Poppy past the cage and see what happens!"

"This I have to see," he said and promptly got the dog and led her past. No squawking and fluster flying, they just carried on chirping happily.

Well, I do believe in miracles and I think that was one, I can't quite believe it worked myself! Helen is now very dear to me, as I am to her. She gave me a brooch that belonged to her mother, which is of a cat, very appropriate, and I know that she will be there if I need help in the mediumship department.

It made me smile so much writing this, firstly, at the absurdity of the whole thing, and, secondly, I know that a little boy will be reading this and at last see his name is in print and maybe, just maybe, one day...

So…"Samuel George Jones, aged seven from Herefordshire - I found that video clip on the internet, clever boy, it is really, really funny! And bless you for taking such good care of your budgies and for having so much more knowledge about the breeds of birds than me or your Mum! Well done you!"

Say Cheese

Whilst working at a holistic fair in Wales, a girl (someone who looked in her mid-twenties, so a girl to me!) had walked past then returned within a short space of time. Her eyes were drawn to my table by the endearing sight of a cuddly black Labrador pup squirming about on my table! It is not that I often have animals 'in the flesh' brought to me, but when they do, it makes a welcome change from just a photograph and this time it did me a big favour.

Having now read my advertising board, this girl, Rhiannon, introduced herself by saying, "Ah, you are just the person I need!" She sat down and I immediately picked up on her sad emotion and said I would do all that I could to help her, and her magnificent Weimaraner, named Cheese. I say 'magnificent' as he was more like a Great Dane in size but certainly not over-cumbersome with it, and was that gorgeous blue-grey colour with such soft amber eyes.

It was not long before the whole distressing tale became apparent and that not only had she been physically bullied by her partner, but the dog had too. She had taken the brave step of leaving her home abroad, and made sure Cheese came too. Her dog was in quarantine although his six month stint was just about finished. She knew he would be overjoyed for them to be re-united but she had some concerns as his life was going to be very different from what he knew and had been used to.

She asked me to explain to him that when she collects him that he would be going to live in a small Welsh cottage at her parents' house, which was not far from the place I was working at that day. "Please apologise to him," she said, "it is so much smaller than the house he has been used to."

With that, he kindly made a valid point, by saying, "Hello? Have you seen the size of my kennel here?!" She chuckled at his response and, to be honest, as he had just spent the last six months in a six-by-ten foot kennel, it really put things into perspective! He was just glad to be getting his freedom back, and starting their new life together. This brought us to the next fear that Rhiannon had - when they lived abroad, it was very rural and where she took him for his walks, or mad runabouts more like, he didn't see any traffic. She was very worried about him and cars, as he was not aware of their danger. I explained to him that there were rules for the cars, but, on the same hand, there were rules for him too, so the two should never meet at the wrong time and place. I did also emphasise the point about what terrible injuries a car can cause and when he had taken this on board, I asked him to offer me a bonding key for Rhiannon to use to remind him of this conversation. It was such a simple one; one word, 'Car!' I made sure she wrote it down (like someone could forget!), but with all the upset in her life, I just wanted to make sure didn't. We covered many other things, and tried to undo the mental damage that may have been caused by being bullied. I was very pleased to tell her that he felt that was in the past and that things were to start afresh again with her and to please stop worrying about him!

We finished the chat and for some reason when she went to pay me, I actually felt impelled to encourage her to take my payment elsewhere - to some healers I knew. She thanked me immensely and went and had a session to help her with her own emotional troubles.

Time went on, as it does, and she often crossed my thoughts and I hoped her life had improved. It had! How lovely is this? We, (Bob and I), moved from Herefordshire to Shropshire, and, Rhiannon found the love of her life in Shropshire too! We then found out that we actually only lived about twelve miles apart! She contacted me and I was delighted to hear that Cheese was very happy, as was she, and completely obeys the 'Car' word! Apparently, if she says it, he comes running back to her and stays by her side until all is safe again. And as she puts it, "This is a dog that, when you call to him to come back, sometimes looks at you with a wild look in his eye and runs in completely the opposite direction! However, yell 'Car' and he comes straight back to me *every* time without fail, stands on the inside of me pressed against my leg and doesn't go until I release him with an 'Okay'. I was amazed; the command, 'Car', was so simple - yet it absolutely works!!"

I now regard Rhiannon as a friend and, as you read in the *Much Ado* story, was invited to her house to meet Cheese in person and his little Westie friend. He is the most delightful dog, as is his owner Rhiannon, and I am so glad I was guided to help her that day in Wales.

Staying Away

When an email comes through with the title, 'Please, please read this', it immediately makes people think that it is 'spam', or maybe one with a internet virus attached. To makes matters worse, the email address consisted of three letters followed by four numbers for their name! I pressed delete then suddenly something made me retrieve it then I opened it with care, and it read:

"Dear Jackie, could you please help me as I have had to re-home my dog. I just can't get over the thought of how much I have hurt him, even though none of it was intentional, and I cry every time I think of him." It continued on to explain...

"Briefly, we moved overseas because of my disability which is made much worse by the British weather. We started up a business and shipped our beloved dog over to us. However, there were unseen problems which meant we had to come back to the UK. We were distraught to find that the vet would not allow Jake to come home with us as his pet passport was missing a vaccination sheet. We tried everything to sort this out - money was never the issue - but finally after eight weeks of badgering between us, our vet in the UK, and the overseas authorities, we had to give up. It seems that the vet had not given Jake a rabies booster even though she had charged us for this and we could prove it. She offered our money back - as if that was ever going to solve anything! Luckily a good friend of ours runs the main animal shelter over on the island and Jake was re-homed with a marvellous family who apparently had fallen in love with him just a few days after he arrived there. They walked him every day and were desperate to adopt him. Eventually they got their wish and took him home. I'm crying as I type this. I would be able to forgive myself a bit if I knew he could understand and knew how much we loved and still love him. If there was ever a chance he could come back to us I would be overjoyed, but I accept that if he is happy where he is then it is right for him to stay. I'm so very distraught over this. I love him so much and need to know that he is happy and can forgive me.

I hope and pray you can reply to me as this is a plea from deep in my heart. Thank you for all you do for us and our animals. Vivienne."

I replied straight back to her as I could now see why I had been 'made to' retrieve this from the Deleted Items folder. I could not quite understand the whole story but told her that I would not charge her for my help in this very sad situation. I then listed what information I needed and also asked if she could let me know where she got my details from. She emailed back and I realised she was referring to the TV show I had been on, as she wrote, "I contacted you immediately as I felt I was meant to see the programme as my husband (a total non-believer and a dedicated 'huffer' whenever I try to watch anything out of the norm) had decided to go off to Tesco's with the kids - a big shock, but a nice surprise!!"

I received a photo of Jake, a beautiful, big, grey Great Dane who is about six years old. Because this reading was 'out of the norm' as he was no longer in her care, I was happy to do it as I knew it was the right thing to do, but phoned her just to get more of an outline and the facts. She explained that they had emigrated to a Caribbean island where her husband had set up a similar business in the construction trade over there. They emigrated along with their four children and settled into the life there. When settled, they arranged for Jake to be exported and, having set everything up in England first, this went according to plan and Jake quickly settled on out there too. Life was brilliant and Vivienne was now no longer totally confined to her wheelchair due to living in sunnier climes. Sadly, everything came to a crashing halt as there was a huge bank collapse on the island and the building trade ceased overnight. They considered every scenario and the only option was for them to return home to Britain. They set about organising Jake's flight home, only to find that the paperwork was not quite as it should be and that was when the question as to whether he had been given his second rabies booster or not. To solve the problem, they had his blood tested to show the immunity level in his system but it failed miserably, so the only conclusion the vets could come to was that he had *not* received his second dose. You would think the answer would be simple – well, give him another or start the course again. Vivienne was prepared to do this and even pay for him to stay on the island for however long it took until he could come back to Britain, but, as his papers were not in order, his passport was declared null and void, and so, in fact, he was an unregistered and unidentifiable dog! They tried in vain to get the authorities to help them, and then after weeks and weeks of trying, surrendered and agreed he would have to be re-homed and live on the island for the rest of his life.

I tuned in with him and said who I was and that I had been asked by Vivienne to chat to him as she desperately wanted to see if he was happy. (At this point, you might think, 'what if he had said he wasn't?' But I just instinctively knew that this wasn't the case, so I knew it was okay to carry on). He was very forward and proved it was him by telling me that he used to try and sit on people's feet, and still does! Knowing the emotional state that Vivienne was in, I passed this news over, and was relieved when she recognised it immediately and said he did. I said I thought we should just let him chat away now, in a way that he wanted. He was very happy and settled and wanted her to remember various things; one of which was the way he had learnt to tuck his jowls behind his canines which came to be known as 'doing the lip'! Apparently he'd even mastered alternating it from one side to the other! Vivienne started to laugh, and said that it was so true and he looked so funny He also said that he didn't enjoy having his nails cut and that he still didn't!! This was his way of trying not to show disloyalty, like - now I have new owners, I have decided I like people cutting my nails – NOT! And he even said that he didn't want her to feel he was being disloyal, but had settled into his new home quite quickly as he knew it was meant to be this way.

Jake then turned the conversation over to Vivienne by telling me that she had a condition that was like 'bones separating at the joints'. To be honest, I had originally presumed it was some type of arthritis she had but asked if his description was correct? And she replied, "Yes it is. I have hip dysplasia!"

I said, "Well, he couldn't be clearer than that, and I think that is him saying, 'Look, I really do remember so much about you and will never forget who you are."

Vivienne asked me to ask him if he was happy with his new family and he told us he was, and that he felt he was there to fill a space. I got the impression that they had lost a child or something along those lines. We were chatting about how he loved the feeling of sand between his toes, and suddenly clear as a bell I heard, "Angel Eyes." I asked if Vivienne recognised this, but she didn't, so I said I definitely heard it, but never mind. We chatted about more and he did everything to let her know that he didn't blame her for a thing and, once again, that it was meant to be this way. I chatted to her and said that I felt that everything in life was going to be the way it was intended, good or bad, but every negative has a positive somewhere.

He interrupted saying, "They talk differently from you, you know."

She laughed and said, "Yes, they would, they are Americans!" Now taking an educated guess, I said I think someone in that house gets called 'Angel Eyes!!'

Jake really wanted her to understand that he remembered the good work she had put into the years she had him, having rescued him at about nine months old and this is what others were now enjoying. He likened this to bringing up a child, who then emigrates and brings joy to others around them. You would be so proud knowing that you had done your best, and knowing what you achieved. Jake also pointed out that Vivienne knew that her children sometimes found her disability frustrating, but to please try and see it as them learning life lessons at an earlier age than most. This should stand them in good stead to be thoughtful and caring to others less fortunate than themselves. Talk about finding a positive!

On another angle, he told me that Vivienne kept asking herself, 'Why, just why had the vet not given him the vaccine as ordered and paid for?' There was no debate on whether she did or didn't (the offer of a refund covered that) but it was eating away at Vivienne, as all this heartache was down to this one vet's actions. Jake was the one who wanted to put a stop to this angst by informing us that it had not been an intentional deceit but just purely lackadaisical and thoughtless. I was quick to let Vivienne know that mistakes have sometimes cost animals their lives and at least he was still alive. I pointed out that the vet has to live knowing the consequence of her actions, and Jake informed us, "This was maybe the big 'kick up the backside' the vet needed!" So we can only hope she will be more responsible in future, because although this animal can never come back home, at least he is still alive.

With Vivienne sounding rather more relieved I asked Jake if he wished to share anything else with us and, with that, he said, "Just look back on this like 'that was a really good time in life, full of fun and laughter, complete with a picture of a pair of knickers on a head!!' The trouble was, I could not make out what type of head these knickers were on, and how was I going to put this one across?!

I started to laugh and said, "I have got a really bizarre picture and, to be honest, I will just say it as it is… did someone, or the kids, put knickers on their, or this dog's head to make people laugh?"

A slight pause (I held my breath) and Vivienne said, "Oh yes, that was my kids. They used to put them on Jake, and, yes, it used to make everyone laugh!" I said that this reminder was served up by Jake for you, and the next time you feel any angst about 'losing' him, just picture those knickers!!

We were nearly finished and I asked if this had helped her, she said it had and that she was just relieved that he was happy and settled. With my work done, I asked Vivienne if there was anything else she would like me to ask before I finished. She said if I didn't mind, could I ask Jake how his leg is? I agreed and asked him to tell me about his leg. He immediately obliged with a picture of him holding up his right front leg and I hoped it was relevant to what she was looking for. Just as she was confirming it was that leg, he 'drew' me an obvious line on it, which to me indicates a break. So I asked if he had broken it although I felt no pain associated with it. She told me that when she had him as a rescue case that it became apparent he had not been fed properly whilst growing. This caused a bone structure problem and he had ended up having a metal plate put in that leg, and that he seemed far better in a warm climate too, as he used to go lame in the damp cold weather. Oh my goodness, we realised what she had unwittingly pointed out - if he was to have come back to England, he would have gradually suffered more and more which would have been terrible for her to watch, and then feel more guilty about coming back to damp, cold Britain. So this 'fate' certainly looked like it had been organised by some form of intervention. Vivienne and I discussed what a dilemma it would have been if she had been forced to make the choice to leave, or not to leave, based on his physical well-being, rather than on one thing that she could not have any say in anyway. She started to think sadly and I said, "Now what have you to think of… knickers!" and with that she laughed! I wished her peace and acceptance and, as sad as a situation as this was, in time everything would slot into place I'm sure. I also said to remember to type a subject heading and not just write, 'Please, please read this' on an email, as chances are, the recipient might not have a cat for a guide to fish it back out again!!

I am so glad that I was able to help this lady as fate had dealt her a cruel hand but I hope that somehow I managed to help ease her pain.

The day after this chat, Vivienne sent me this lovely email that I have also asked her permission to include:

Dear Jackie,

Thank you so so much for speaking to me and Jake yesterday. I have to apologise for being less than chatty but as I'm sure you knew I was crying the whole way through. I had a good think about everything that was said and, last night was the first time I thought about Jake without welling up. I think the stuff we went through is going to be a massive help to me and really the gratitude I feel for you cannot be conveyed by words alone. You are so special and I'm so honoured that you helped me in this way.

Many many thanks
Love Vivienne.

P.s. It was very kind of you not to charge me for the reading so I will be making a donation to the Great Dane Rescue (seems appropriate). Thank You.

"I am not brave of heart."
The first words from a horse when I asked him to tell me something about himself. He was such a sincere horse but found most things in life a worry.

"I'm not clumsy; I just don't look where I am going!"
A lovely Labrador explaining his 'goofiness'.

"It is just a place for people to leave their names."
A very philosophical statement from a dog that often visits a graveyard with her owner. A good one to ponder; I think those few words explain the difference from the physical being to the spiritual being.

"I think I snore. Can you ask them if I really do?!"
A lovely question from a dog for his owners, and their answer was an emphatic 'YES!!'

A Cruel Departure

I had spent a lovely few hours at one yard chatting to three horses, well, one pony and two horses to be precise. They were all so different; the pony was the family pet and a cheeky but honourable little chap. One horse had a 'I'd rather do it my way or not at all' attitude, but the other was the crème de la crème of horses, he'd had been there, done it and got the tee-shirt! He chatted about his previous home where he had competed at top level. It is not often that horses show me bottles of champagne, but he did, coupled with rows and rows of red rosettes. He also showed me a picture of the biggest and poshest of horse boxes you would ever see! But, saying all that, he was having a more sedate life now, and was totally adored by his present owner. He told us that really loved this personal home which was far more endearing to him than a professional yard.

I was now at the next call and standing in front of a young mare called Cinnamon, aptly named after her roan colour. I was quite surprised as it seemed I was going to be doing the communication with her husband rather than the lady who had booked it. I don't mean to sound sexist, but men normally tend to be very sceptical unless they have experienced it personally. My luck was in, her owners had done communication before with someone else so knew how it worked and what to expect. I tuned in with this youngster who was rising five, and immediately was bombarded with this angst. She made me feel like I wanted to stamp my feet, and shout and cry like a child, 'Why me, why me, it is all so unfair!' I passed this over, and the owner nodded, saying that was her to a tee. Just at that point his wife appeared, introduced herself and I said I would just let Cinnamon rant and see why she felt like this. The mare went on and on, and said she was not awkward, although people thought it of her, and this turned out to be mainly about her breaking process. The problem was, yes she was tricky, yes she was rather awkward but, unfortunately, an old joint injury was starting to hurt again. So this unwillingness to work because of discomfort, but unfortunately looked like more behavioural problems. She was talking at speed, saying things to me as fast as I could repeat them, but we established that there was a problem breaking and, in the end, she had come home.

The next picture was of her hurtling round and round a stable but she looked like a foal. She then said, "Oh, I miss my mum, where is my mum?"

His wife looked so crestfallen, she uttered, "I knew it was about this, my sister has always said the same." I got the background and, sadly, someone had recommended their method of weaning which was to take mother out of the stable, hold the foal back, and shut all doors! Well, the obvious happened, this poor foal just screamed and cried for days. This set up terrible anxieties and a lack of trust in people, because if they can take away the most precious thing – her mum – then what else were they capable of? The owner felt dreadful and had realised that this was a big mistake and has never done it like that since. I hear a lot of similar stories and try to tell people, think of it like you yourself. Say, for example; the one you love has to leave you and go and live abroad - you would not like it, but if you had been told and had the time to get used to it, you would take that opportunity to say all you wanted to and in the end learn to accept it. Or, on the other hand, would you like to have it this way? - You go into the house you have shared for months and whilst you are upstairs, someone drags her off. You come downstairs and you find there is… nothing! What's happened?! You cry, 'Is she okay, did she run away, does she not want me anymore? Please someone tell me when I will see her again?' Done like that, do you think you would hear any answers? No, and the sad thing is people can't hear these innocents that are shouting the questions.

By now we had told Cinnamon her mother was well and this had been a mistake. She understood but said that she didn't think she would be able to work because of her leg problem. She showed me what looked like a curve in a bone, and this turned out to be where she had been operated on her hock, but, sadly, riding had actually caused inflammation in this damaged joint. Her owners asked me to ask her what she wanted in life. Her answer - not to be ridden, but as she was very good looking and was well bred, she would love to have babies for them. It was promised there and then that next year she would visit the stallion and try for a foal and of course, thanks to this sad learning curve, the weaning would be done in the most thoughtful and least stressful way possible.

A Gem of a Tale

This little story I could not leave out as it is just so sweet and you couldn't make it up. In the majority of the stories in this book I use the real names of animals and their owners. This one is the same and you will see why I couldn't be anything else!

I had a long chat with Sheena's horse called Cash who was such a hoot to talk to. He had so much to say for himself, and was truly adored. He spoke of all the various things he and Sheena did and boasted about his extreme speed – well, according to him anyway! Sheena agreed that he could 'shift', and on hearing that comment he stated, "From now on, I think I should be known as Cash and Dash!" My sides and jaw hurt from chatting with him, and Sheena said her mare would be the next one for me to talk to.

A few weeks later, a picture of Camilla appeared. Yes, Camilla, I have never heard of another horse with that name, a rather unusual choice I think you would agree. She was far more reserved than her mate 'Cash and Dash', and was very much a ladies ride, gentle and thoughtful and was the apple of Sheena's eye. We talked about various things and, thanks to 'matey' above, she also wanted a word about her name. She said that although she had been 'christened' Camilla, she too would rather be called something else.

"What would you like to be called then?" we asked.

"Gem," she replied, and launched into her own explanation. "Gem, as in a gem of a horse, I think that is me. Don't you?"

"Absolutely," declared Sheena, "so okay, Gem it is!"

I thanked them for the chat, and thought what a wonderful pair of horses, that were truly loved for their own different ways. Sheena has been wonderful at recommending me and I have met some very nice animals and people through her.

Two days later I got a phone call from Sheena who was so excited (and baffled at the same time) that I could just about make out the, "...and I just had to tell you!" bit. Sheena then explained to me, at a slightly slower speed, that she had gone to her in-laws house that night and there on the table was a dog tag with the name GEM on it. The strange thing was, they didn't have a dog named that, nor could anyone recall ever having one! How the tag got there we will never know, but it now adorns the bridle of a mare now newly christened, Gem!

Moving On

You know in life when things are just flowing along so happily, then suddenly the tide turns and you are left feeling like your heart will break. The next two stories are an example of that so maybe allow yourself time for a quiet moment to reflect afterwards.

In the summer of 2009 I was contacted by Traci, the owner of two horses, Pinkie and Gus. Pinkie was nearly thirty years old, a cremelo pony that was cream coloured like the name suggests. However, Gus, her horse, took great delight in pointing out that Pinkie, as a name, was obviously not quite accurate then was it?! We giggled at this and did not bother to explain that she had (as they do) a very pink muzzle and eyelids to match. Gus, affectionately known as Gussie, was twenty-four, a handsome deep mahogany bay, who was once a Grade A show jumper.

Traci came to me for a reading for Gus, and what fun we had. Yes he had physical problems, but had a great sense of humour and such a warm, sunny demeanour. Although I spend my time saying to people: "Don't worry they won't say things I shouldn't hear," he did enlighten me to some slightly colourful language used by Traci, but never directly at him, I hasten to add!! He would never (as animals don't) have mentioned it unless it was harmless and inoffensive, but he just wanted to drop Traci in it for sheer entertainment value. He informed us that just because she was behind the stables, don't think they couldn't hear her mutterings from there! Traci was the type of client I love; really down to earth, honest and full of fun, and most importantly, adored her horses. She found this hilarious that he had noticed, and said that she would try and not do it so much, well, within his earshot anyway! I just found this was amusing, as did Gussie. He also took great pleasure in informing her that he knew she was trying to cover up medicine in his food and that is why he would not take it! He said that if she actually told him what it was for, then he might be okay about it, and later she told me, he was!! He was so sweet, and knew that Traci would spend her last penny on both him and Pinkie, and asked me to tell her how much he loved her and appreciated all that she did.

We covered many things, like the problems he was having with his feet and his pelvis, age related stuff, but in general he was a happy lad who liked to make Traci smile. Throughout the reading, he repeatedly let it be known that Traci could 'hear', in the same clairaudient (the proper term for hearing) way like I do. Due to his persistence, I eventually said to her, "I think that you hear things too, don't you?"

There was a slight pause, then an admission, "Yes, but my boyfriend thinks I'm mad!"

"Well, you are not," I assured her, and then informed her, "I am being told that you have been given this, as you have gone to extreme lengths to help animals. Do you understand what that means?" It turned out Traci had travelled hundreds of miles to rescue Pinkie and was just one of those genuine caring girls who had gone to extraordinary lengths to animals needing help. The spirit world often recognise this, and want those people to be able to do even more by helping in the way I do. With the help of spirit, the work can spread far and wide as they have access to everyone and anywhere, whereas our physical bodies, when it comes to helping animals worldwide, are a severe limitation.

As we were finishing the lovely reading, Pinkie did get a mention from Gussie, who was under the impression her eyesight was 'none too clever', but apart from that, they were 'happy as Larry'. Traci knew that I was trying to get my first book published and asked me to let her know when I did, so I promised I would.

A few months later, in September, I was travelling back down from Wales and a message 'beeped' up on my mobile. I listened and it was Traci, extremely distressed, saying that Pinkie had died, and Gus was beside himself - please could I help.

I called her as soon as I got home, and it turned out that Pinkie had died three days previously. Gus was still 'screaming' and running up and down, in spite of everything that Traci was doing to try and help him and just wouldn't settle. Traci was so frightened he would either injure himself, or go down with stress colic. I tuned in with him, and he was totally distraught. I suddenly got a 'thump thump' feel on my chest, which normally indicates a heart attack to me, and Traci confirmed that Pinkie, according to her vets, had died from one. Gus was so very upset and told us that he had known for the whole of the previous week that she had a problem. This was shown to me by him, 'shadowing' her by following her around the paddock. Traci recognised this and said that she had not known why he was doing it, but then you wouldn't would you. So, if he had known that she was going to pass over, then why was he so distraught? The reason was; he had been waiting and waiting for it to happen and be there to share in her last seconds of this life, when in fact what happened was, during that night he had dozed off and when he had woken up she had already passed away. Oh bless him, he was so dreadfully upset and I set about trying to calm him down and see if I could make things better for him. He asked if he could have sliced apples to be given to him, arranged in Pinkie's feed bowl. Traci said that he was not really fond of apples, but I said I thought as he had asked for them to make it anyway. He showed me he wanted them like an 'apple flan' look, so would be like a pretty and personal present from Pinkie. Just as we had got that organised, another little voice 'popped in' – Pinkie's. I realised straight away that it was her, and she was reassuring Gus and Traci that she was fine, and had felt nothing and please, try not to be sad. She then said that she could help Traci from there, because Traci can 'hear' and she would be the one to help her, now she had moved to the next world. I told Traci this and she mumbled, "Oh I don't know if I would be able to, I don't think I would be good enough."

A little voice said to ask her, "Would she say that I (Pinkie) was honest and true?"

"Oh yes, without doubt," was Traci's emphatic reply.

And then Pinkie said, "So please tell her that I am here for her, and I will always be honest and true, and help guide her and work with her." Traci was very tearful, but suddenly felt empowered by the thought that she could really look into communicating and thanked Pinkie, and me, for our efforts. (If I come across people that I find out are clairvoyant, I do try to encourage them as one, I feel it is my duty to get more help out there, and secondly, it is the most wonderful feeling to be able to do the work we do.)

I wished her all the best with Gussie and hoped that now we had all heard from Pinkie, and that his request would be covered, that he would settle back down, and sure enough by the next day he was so much calmer.

A few weeks later she emailed me to let me know that Gus was totally back to normal and added, in her own words, "Hi Jackie, I got your book and it is amazing!! I will do a review for you as soon as I finish it, but a certain little pony interrupts me as soon as I start to read it!!" I thought that was lovely and truly showing that Pinkie is determined to try and get her to start communicating and listening to what she could hear.

Within weeks, I got the saddest email – One afternoon, Traci had felt drawn to go down to the yard (guided by Pinkie I am sure) and heard Gus calling. She dropped everything, she just knew something was wrong (of course she would) and found he was down on the ground, and could not get up. She phoned the vet and as much as they tried she knew there and then, he was going to leave this world too and be re-united with Pinkie. Devastated was not the word, nothing could describe the loss she felt and I did my best to comfort her, but a grieving process needs to be done to help us learn to live here, without the ones we still love.

I did not hear anything from her for a little while, but on the very day that I had decided to brave it, and go and ask for spirit animals to come through (Phoebe and Connie from the Much Ado about Everything story). I had finished that phone call, and half an hour later the phone rang. A familiar voice on the other end, Traci, and without thinking I said, "How are you?"

With that, she just dissolved into tears, and said, "I know you don't go asking, but as Pinkie had come through to you, I just wondered…" I immediately said that I would try and explained that I had mentioned her to the last lady whose two spirit dogs had been a pivotal point in my work, and that I would call her back in half an hour. At the point of me saying that, I could see Gussie doing the most fantastic 'sliding stops' in a field, and made me feel like laughing, and Traci said, "Yes that's him!"

I didn't even have to ask for Gussie to come through, he was ready and waiting, and full of himself. He was jumping and kicking, saying, "Look, they all work again, it's great!" He assured Traci that he was fine and told me, "That half hour was so special." I asked Traci if she understood it, and she did. She had sat with him for half an hour whilst waiting for the vet to arrive, with his head in her lap and talked to him sharing that beautiful last physical time together. Confirming that it was really him was the fact that she had asked him to give her love to Pinkie when he arrived - this was exactly what Traci had said. Gussie was determined that this chat was to be a moment of joy, not gloom, and made us roar with laughter with his gentle expressive sarcasm, "Oh, I have got Pinkie here now," with the air of, 'oh, here you are, and about time too!' "Nothing has changed you know," he declared, "she is still just as lazy!!" This was so spot on. I actually never really knew Pinkie, but a lazy little soul apparently she was. Gus then said his goodbyes, and said that Traci now had them both to help her, so please would she try!! She agreed, and said that for them she would.

Traci has told me since that she has been looking into learning the ins and outs of what we communicators do. I know that when the time is right, she will be wonderful; after all, with Gus and Pinkie behind her, she cannot fail. They have shown me, once again, that souls just move to a different world, and from there, there are no obstacles, physical or mental, so they really are in a position to help us here on Earth. And do you know the lovely thing? They really want to. In this job you have to have compassion, honesty, a good sense of humour, and most of all a very good guide, and you know what - she has them all.

Two Little Boys

I feel we are put in the right place, at the right time for a reason, although, at this point I felt I really didn't want to be there. I had been booked to do a charity evening at a fairly local pub raising good funds for the cancer unit and demonstrating the art of animal communication. Sadly, the proceedings were blighted by one individual who took great pleasure in 'blanking' all that I said. Then by another lady who seemed very uncomfortable about anything I tried to say about her horse.

I brought the evening to an abrupt halt, feeling much deflated, downhearted and was reduced to tears. This was upsetting to say the least and my confidence hit an all time low. Believe me, it is no easy task to stand up there in public and do this, hoping with every bone in your body that you are right. The 'blanker' had got his ignorant pleasure out of it; how, I will never understand, because others present were agreeing with the facts I was giving as they knew him and his horses too! I find this behaviour so appalling because in such cases as this it is not just me they are taunting but their own animals as well!

The lady, however, was a very different story and had a genuine reason for 'batting away' everything I said from her mare. I had, in between, managed to talk to a lovely dog and managed to show that communication is genuine and I was not some fraud putting myself in the firing line to raise funds for charity. I will give the club their due; they still gave me the cheque for the cancer unit, so at least I had achieved that.

By now, I had fled the room and taken refuge in the bar area where I was quickly tracked down by this lady and her friend, apologising profusely. She explained that she had not understood the concept that they could actually talk and as, sadly, her mare was shortly going to Heaven, she could not bear for this to be announced to all in attendance. She admitted that everything I had told her matched with her mare, so she knew what I was doing was genuine, so then panic had ensued. I told her not to worry and asked if she would like to take this opportunity to talk to her horse, and maybe put both their minds at rest about her impending departure. The lady bravely took me up on this offer, with her dear friend sitting there for support and comfort.

This animal was in her late teens and had serious physical problems, causing her difficulties in getting up and down. She was very good at telling 'how it was' and very accurate with the medical terminology too. The mare was sad but relieved to be going as she was never going to improve and did not want to lose complete quality of life. Her owner thanked me and did something that astounded me - She went back into the room filled with the people discussing what had occurred and announced that I had actually been extremely accurate and had just told her exactly what was wrong with her mare. She also continued further by to explain about her previous actions towards me. I truly say thank you to this lady, she could have walked away and not said a word but chose the path of valour and defended me, in spite of her own emotional pain.

Sharing the emotional situation was this dear lady, Jean, who sadly had had her eight month old puppy stolen from her a year previously and was broken hearted but still searching in earnest. She did approach me about trying a missing pet task but, as I have explained before, I do not get involved with these kinds of emotional turmoil, as sadly, a high percentage are never found and even if 'located' cannot be tracked down in time.

A year must have passed, and on a Saturday lunchtime, Jean, who had remembered me from that rather odd charity evening, contacted me asking for urgent help with a young whippet called Jake. Time was of the essence, so she immediately sent me through a picture of this gorgeous four year old, fawn and white Whippet. He looked simply divine, sitting on his blanket in the boot area of her car. As soon as the phone call started, I instantly started to feel bloated with severe pain accompanying it, like my guts had gone into spasm, and feeling ready to burst with it. I put this carefully and gently to Jean and she confirmed that is exactly how she would describe what was happening. I delved deeper and I also described a rather odd picture, with a bit of reticence I might add, of finger-like flanges inside his gut. Jean again recognised this and explained to me that he had been diagnosed with Lymphangiectasia. This is thought to be a congenital condition that basically causes these growths in the gut which then impede the passing of their stools.

Jean is very holistic and, although sought conventional medicine in the shape of high doses of steroids, painkillers etc. from the vet, found a healer who helped Jake's bloated body reduce back down in size. The vets even agreed to reduce the steroids and painkillers and, for a few months, it looked as if she was maybe going to get her Jake back after all. He had far more energy and exuberance but, sadly, this was to be his downfall. Being a whippet, his rabbit catching instincts kicked back in and a feast was to be had. He ran like the wind, far into the distance and landed his prey, devouring all that he could before Jean could get to him and take it away.

For such a princely prize, a huge sum was to be paid. For a dog whose diet had been so carefully managed, his gut intolerance went into overdrive. These growth flanges were causing blockages and his system ceased to flow, so the onset of pain was intense. He had deteriorated so fast that he had received veterinary treatment and was at this point attached to a drip. Rather than him being kept at the surgery, they allowed him into Jean's care, so now she was sitting with him, trying to reassure him and hold a conversation with me. So, in his presence, this sad phone call Jean decided she needed to have to give Jake, the opportunity to say exactly what he wanted.

There was the option of an operation to remove the blockages and parts of his intestines which I conveyed to him. He didn't even pause to answer this; he informed us these abnormalities would just keep coming back so there was no point. Did he want to go and see the healer, was the second question. Although he was very grateful for the work his healer had done, Jake said that this was way beyond that now. At this point, I could hear him crying in the background and, as sometimes does happen, I was overcome with emotion and reduced to tears myself.

He then very clearly said, well, begged actually, "Please let me go, I really want to go. I have had enough." With tears streaming down Jean's face, she held him and said she would phone the vet immediately and give him his wish. Jake asked me to thank Jean with all his heart and said he had been, 'Mummy's little soldier and that's the way it was meant to be.' We finished the call and I sent all the love and strength I could muster to help Jean and him through this.

The phone rang around five o'clock and it was Jean to let me know that he had 'gone' now and was out of pain. She understandably was extremely upset but, being the wonderful lady she is, had the heart to let me know as she had involved me in this emotional situation too.

I can truly say I was deeply touched and, how she had the strength to call me I will never know.

Like the story above, it is a sad fact that many times in our own lifetime we will suffer the heartbreak of our animals going to Heaven. Something we don't often hear or think about is an owner dying and leaving the pet needing a new home. Sadly the owner of Tigger, who was Jean's other Whippet, had suddenly died leaving Tigger urgently needing a new home which is how he came to live with Jean. A few years later, a friend of Jean's, who owned a gorgeous blue Whippet, admired Tigger and thought it would be lovely if they could breed a litter from the pair. Jean agreed and so they waited for the bitch to come into season. Very sadly, the owner died unexpectedly, but when her bitch came into season very soon afterwards, the lady's husband felt that they should go ahead and fulfil her wishes. The result - Jake and nine others! What a wonderful legacy of a friendship.

Although father and son, with Tigger five years senior, they played and bounced about like two kids and the balance was slightly restored. As you have read, this was not to last and, although Tigger was extremely sad, we talked to him and he assured us that Jake was now out of pain and just gone to another place. He also wanted to report on Jake's spiritual visit. He relayed the conversation from the house when Jean thought her husband had opened the back door and he thought vice versa. I reminded her of the conversation and she laughed and said it was spot on but what was it relevant to? Tigger explained that it was Jake visiting and that the door was not properly closed so he had pushed it wide open to make his presence known. Jean immediately remembered the 'bunting' feeling on the back of her leg, another one of Jake's little personal touches. He had not made his presence so overtly aware since but I hear it so often, including us humans too, that they come back to say a last goodbye. In my own opinion, I tend to think this is actually also confirming to the spirit that they really have passed over and are no longer a physical being, so can then move on spiritually. As I have explained before, although they have left the ones they loved down here, they are meeting many loved ones who had gone to Heaven before them.

Tigger was not without his own physical problems too. He was quick to pass me a strange pins and needles feeling from his right back foot and this was associated with the accident from a few years previously. When I say accident, a very serious spinal injury, causing severe damage to his top two vertebrae. I asked him to show me how he had done it and he showed me him running full pelt then going head over heels and landing badly on his neck. It turns out this wasn't the first time he had tried to 'brake' when the impulsion of his body had carried on, so it all made sense and another mystery solved.

Jean explained to me that after Tigger's spinal surgery he was paralysed for three months and completely dependent on her and her husband for everything. Now some people reading this might think 'how awful to keep a dog going in that predicament' but if you have met someone like Jean then you would understand what total devotion and dedication meant. Some of us can cope with situations like that, others can't, but that doesn't make either of us right or wrong, just different. She did all that was needed and within three months, he had recuperated enough to start moving about and very well, considering the invasive surgery he had gone through.

So this conversation was taking place a few months further on and, although he was so much better, he was still not right. She had gone through every check possible but nothing was found that could be medically pinpointed. Mind you, if you think about it, a pins and needles feeling, this would be very hard to find, let alone explain. I asked him why he thought it was occurring and he simply explained that there was nerve damage so things were not flowing as they should and that acupuncture was the way to go. I recommended a vet to her (bizarrely, there is a rule that only vets can do acupuncture on animals, which takes some understanding as there are some fantastic acupuncturists out there that do nothing but acupuncture, day in and day out) that I knew of that had a good reputation. Jean contacted her and she ethically said she needed a referral and, unbelievably, Jean's own practice did acupuncture too, just didn't advertise the fact!

Tigger had two treatments and then we had a chat. The change was remarkable, he could feel more strength and flow in that leg and the pins and needles were diminishing. Also, as a bonus, because acupuncture often treats more than just the area concerned, he reported that his breathing was better and this was from a higher oxygen flow. So, great news all round and a good indication of how alternative therapies can do amazing work, like it also did for Teddy in the *Getting the Needle* story The more cases with positive outcomes from alternative treatments like acupuncture, the more vets might push it to the fore - well, here's hoping anyway!

Tigger is now running round like a two year old again and I do hope he has learnt how to work his 'brakes' and will have many more happy and painless years ahead of him.

I was fortunate enough to meet up with Jean not long ago at a local country show. She is a lady that is so full of heart and not just for the animals but people too. Had she not offered to share the burden of emotion with her friend who was about to lose her sweet mare, she might not have thought of me. I was honoured to be allowed to help with Jake's passing and to improve Tigger's quality of life too. These two little boys had been through courageous battles in their own individual way and I thank Jean, as I am sure they both do, for the love and strength of courage she has shown.

~~~~~

From my first book many people mentioned to me that my *Letting Go* poem had helped ease their hearts after having gone through the sadness like in the previous two stories. Spirit helped me to write it to say from them about the different aspects of a passing. These words have helped people come to terms with their loss and gave them some peace and understanding. I have, therefore decided to put it in this book too and intend to include it in every book I write as making such a painful decision is sadly a part of most animal lover's lives. Over the page you will find my words that I hope will spread far and wide and help bring some light into those with a heavy heart.
~~~~~

Letting go

Your heart is bursting, searing with pain
That physical touch never to be had again
You only let them go because you so clearly care
They might not be here but they are surely up there

You feel the pull and the tear of your heart
You feel torn inside and ripped apart
The enormity of choosing what best to do
It was done with your love, as they looked to you

We don't enter into this without thought or care
We do it because the compassion is there
The choice to stop pain and distress of the one we love
Can only be guided by you and the angels above

Many spirits have come through and given me their word
Your tears of sorrow and distress they heard
But they are free and happy and hold no ill will
Whatever was wrong could not have been cured with a pill

The height of pain is a measuring device
It shows how deeply you felt throughout their life
With your love given for this most selfless act
They at least left this earth with their heart intact

Now up yonder and free to roam
This is another level, like a new home
The day will come when you go up there too
They're ready and waiting to meet and embrace you

If you truly did this from your genuine heart
You were so brave and helped them depart
Your love and courage was seen from above
This really was your strongest act of love

Animal Talking Tales

If you could ask them now, what might they say?
"In my life, that was actually only one single day,
Please remember the rest, the joy, love and play,
For I look down from above and remember it that way."

As time has passed you may at last feel some ease
Maybe a pet has come for you to please
Animals are not selfish and want you to share
They left that space for another needing your love and care

We are truly honoured to share in their space
Think back and let that smile adorn your face
The precious time you had could never be measured
Your lasting memories are of those you truly treasured

Jackie and Rolf
2009

On a Wing and a Prayer

I believe that in life we are on set paths that we are to follow, so to try and walk them as best as we can. They may lead you to sadness or to utter joy and, for me, this one was leading me to a Falconry in Stratford upon Avon. This joyous occasion was to fulfil a lifelong ambition of mine; to hold a bird of prey, (I had never in my wildest dreams thought about talking to one!), and this all became possible thanks to my dear friend, Pam. She also was in my first book with her delicate Lurcher, Marigold, and at about the same time as the chat with her dog, I also did a communication for her friend's dog and horse. Sadly, within a year, the dog and horse had both gone to Heaven, and even more tragically, their owner followed. She suffered a very sudden onset of illness that she was never going to be able to recover from. On her path in life, she left a gorgeous daughter Becky, and Becky's passion in life is falconry. This is something I have admired all my life, and now I had a personal invite from her to go and talk to the birds at the centre she was running.

I can truly say I had no preconceived ideas of what might and might not happen, I was so excited. Bob and I travelled down, armed with video camera for this very special occasion and, for once in our lives, found the place without our usual 'round the houses' detour!

Becky met us in the foyer and took us down to meet her dogs, (one of whom I had chatted to) and the wide selection of birds, complete with a baby falcon in the office. Becky has vast experience of demonstration flying and explaining to an audience all the different things they do, and why they do it. So, armed with her pad and paper, we headed off to see the birds.

First in the line, sitting on her perch, was Marge. She was a magnificent Harris Hawk, of a beautiful deep mahogany colour with a vivid yellow beak and a dash of white through her tail. Until this day, I had never had a bird of prey perch on my wrist, but with some instruction, and a very thick glove, here I was doing it. I must say, she really did feel very heavy, and as much as Becky said, "Just relax your arm, you will get used to it," I wasn't finding that the easiest thing to do!

As I had no idea what to ask them, I thought I would just let them say what they wanted. I asked Marge what she would like to tell us, and she impressed upon us her self-importance, and her wonderful flying skills. She announced, "I was two and a half today!" which totally confused me, but apparently was what she had weighed that morning! I couldn't quite get the concept, so Becky explained that every day they are weighed, as their flying weight is crucial. In short, as far as I gathered, they are kept at a certain weight, because if they get 'too heavy' they get lazy and won't fly. The reason they want to fly is to hunt, and this is to chase the lure (something on the end of a line simulating a moving target) to catch food, so when they come back to their falconer, they get rewarded with a piece of food.

So, having listened and got that straight, and bearing in mind this was being filmed, I turned to Becky and asked, "Is that two and a half kilos or two and a half pounds?" Well, Bob erupted with laughter, and said, "Jackie, if she was two and a half kilos, I hardly think you would be able to hold her on your wrist!" Good point, but this metric conversion sometimes does get the better of me! However, to put this into perspective, it would be the equivalent of me balancing the weight of two oven ready chickens on my wrist! Marge finished off by telling me that sometimes she liked to jump off her perch and 'squawk' at other birds down the line! This, Becky was unsure about, and said that she didn't think she had seen her do that. Never mind, it was a fun chat, and I had learnt a great deal already.

We moved along and I chatted to various others, and it was amazing the diversity between birds; some were very cheeky, and others quite arrogant and even try to give their handler a hard time! There was one very funny bird, Hector, who knew 'the game' inside out and would purposely 'disobey' by landing on the ground near the children, which would cause tumultuous laughter amongst them. He would then hop along the ground like a robin, back to the handler. This 'on the ground milarky' being totally the opposite of any content in a training book but hilarious to see, but when he flew properly, he was a whiz to watch.

Next I talked to a female Saker Hawk, and Becky told us how these birds fly at such phenomenal speeds and actually hunt by 'crashing' their feet into the heads of large prey, like a gazelles for example. This is similar to being hit by a bullet at 200+ miles per hour!

In some countries they are trained to do this, and work with hunters to get meals for themselves and their families.

Next to her was the smallest and sweetest looking little bird I have ever seen. She was a Merlin who was ten years old, and had spent her whole life in captivity as a breeding bird. I learnt that breeding birds don't ever go out and fly, and are fed more so they produce eggs. She was now at this flying centre, by the genuine kindness of someone who had purchased her a year previously from her original breeder/owner. The horrible fact was during her 'breeding years', is that this tiny bird was being artificially inseminated with a syringe! How it did not cause her severe damage over the years was a miracle. But saying that, this bird was a prime example of 'accepting her lot' in life, as she knew no different, so held no malice or upset about it. I mentioned she had been purchased, and for a great sum I might add (this is serious financial business), but the gentleman concerned could not bring himself to inflict such discomfort on one so small and beautiful. So after a year, he agreed to sell her for a nominal price to Becky, who would see if she could train her to become a demonstration flying bird.

This little Merlin Hawk had been named Mary, although not because they thought a 'regal' name would suit her; she actually was named after one of the helper's girlfriends, who was very pretty but also very 'mouthy' with it. I had to laugh, but for such a little bird, she sure could talk above the rest of them! We talked about why she struggled when being held (for beak cutting etc.) and she said it made her think the worst was about to happen again. We promised her 'the fertilising' was now in the past and Becky said she would repeat these assurances during any treatment to try to help her relax. Becky also mentioned that they could see she was fearful when they took her out to teach her the flying routine, and 'could I ask why and what could we do to help'. It was nothing to do with the routine, she just felt very vulnerable, thinking that large prey birds would be able to catch her. We explained, that could never happen, and ask the other birds here, they will tell you that wild prey birds would not dare come near.

Becky and I kept in touch, and she told me that Mary had overcome her fears and was flying and loving it! I mentioned to Becky to check out my website, as I had put up a banner of pictures of Marge and me. The funniest thing that sticks in my mind was just at the end of my bird talking day, when Marge jumped off her perch, squawked very loudly, as if to validate her earlier remark. I laughed, gave her the 'thumbs up' and said, "Thanks, Marge!"

Oh, So Boring!

The joy of my work is made all the more pleasurable by the difference between animals and the unusual behaviour that I am sometimes witness to. I was on a yard and had chatted to two lovely horses. One was just the most wonderful boy, so sweet and genuine and if I could have fitted him in my pocket, I would have taken him home! The other was a very mixed-up horse that was, at that point, in the stages of recovery from a serious illness too. He told me that 'his colour had saved him', which, sadly, turned out to be the truth. He had been through many homes but as he was such a 'well-marked' coloured horse that had kept his value up, in spite of all his behavioural problems.

Having finished talking to them, the owner of the yard took me over to see her mare that Bob had just finished dental work on. I introduced myself to 'Rosie', as we shall call her, and asked her to tell me something about herself. Well, her response had all the excitement of someone going to a chiropodist; I had to really 'push' to get her to join in! Had she been the first horse, I would have been worried that I looked like I couldn't really talk to them after all. Fortunately as the first two were like 'chalk and cheese' and their owner had shed a few tears of joy and sadness, Rosie's owner, Jane, knew I was genuine.

I asked Rosie what she liked and I got a brief answer saying that she could jump. I asked another couple of things and she came across as very 'workman-like' and was just doing her job, being a horse, and was happy with that. I said to her owner that she was very hard to talk to, and Bob was also listening and admitted later that he felt sorry for me as it seemed an uphill battle. She had no complaints and was not unhappy, so I decided to ask her, as I do all animals, what was her favourite sign of love/affection? "A couple of pats on my neck will do!" was her unemotional reply.

Jane, said, "Yes, that's our Rosie, she does not do affection!" Then Rosie gave me a real 'ice-breaker'. She proceeded to lie down in front of us, complete with nose resting on the floor, shut her eyes and went to sleep! Well, we laughed and Jane said, "Oh look, you have bored her to sleep, but joking apart, this is what she is like!" I felt relieved as Jane had not expected anything less of her although she had not done exactly this before.

It is so unusual for a horse to step back from someone who is paying them attention, simply lie down facing that person and so obviously go straight to sleep, just as if nobody was there! To be honest, Bob and I were quite worried as she was making some strange noises, and horses that have colic do lie down and grunt and groan. It was obviously that she was sound asleep which a colic horse certainly wouldn't be. Again Jane reassured us that she had heard those sounds from her before, so we stopped worrying. It was just so bizarre, but I guess if she was a person, she would be the one in a corner with a book, head down in their own little world.

Jane had owned Rosie since she was a yearling and knew her well. All the information I had managed to encourage out of her was correct but there was one problem that I really struggled to get the answer to - When Rosie was standing in a showing line-up she would, for no apparent reason, suddenly start tilting and shaking her head, and once she started, she would not stop. This had cost her a couple of wins, and as she had a big competition coming up could I please find out why? Needless to say, she did not volunteer this behaviour, so I tried a different tack and asked her what she thought of showing. She, in her few short words, said that some of the classes were so big that it took ages, and so she was bored! Jane said that the last time it happened there were forty in that class but as the next show was a championship - if she could resist showing her boredom, they would have a really good chance. Five minutes later, I eventually got some words from her for Jane to say to remind her how important the occasion was and to keep still. I passed them over and Jane wrote them down but, to be honest, I was not sure they would be worth the paper they were written on. Anyway, I had done my best and I now felt mentally exhausted.

Bob packed his dental kit away and I wished her luck and said, "If it does work, please let me know and, by the way, where are you competing?"

"At Olympia", she replied, (all the horsey folk will recognise that name as Olympia is the horse equivalent of the footballers' F.A. Cup match).

"Wow, Olympia!" I said, "I can now see why this occasion is so important, best of luck!!"

Jane phoned me the next week to let me know they had been placed in the top ten, which was a fabulous result for them, and she was delighted. Jane said she had used the words and there was no head shaking! But, to be honest, we will never know if this was sheer luck or if Rosie had listened to a word I said. If I was a betting person, I would go for the 'sheer luck' BUT, if a bookmaker was going to offer me decent odds on a horse lying down and going to sleep like she did, I'd take him up on it. I reckon the chances of me seeing another horse blatantly 'switch off' like that would be pretty slim!

At the end of the day, this mare was happy with life in her own way. And, even with her lack of human interest, to have qualified for, and then been placed at Olympia, she must have had to sparkle at quite a few places to get noticed in the first place.

Last Ditch Attempt

Tiffany, a riding instructor, is one of our long-standing dental clients. On a previous occasion whilst out with Bob, I had a chat with a mare she had at the time. My memory fails me on most of the conversation, but I do remember her to be a really loving mare, and that she was actually only on loan to Tiffany, (Tiff as she is known to everyone). When asked if there was anything she wanted to say to Tiff, she told us that, 'Tiff's pupils thought she was strict, but fair!!" I passed that one over carefully and Tiff smiled and said, "I would agree with that!"

Having experienced my work first hand, when Tiff hit problems with her new horse, Arnie, the first person she thought to call was me. Arnie is a Thoroughbred; a stunning, bright bay, with dark points that apparently Tiff had been trying for two years to buy from a racing trainer she had worked for. At the age of seven, they eventually agreed to sell him to her, and if anyone knows her horses, Tiff does.

Re-schooling ex-racehorses takes a lot of time and a lot of skill to do it properly. For a start, which I learnt to my cost, when you change your hands, (alter your reins) on a cantering racehorse, they don't slow down, they get faster. This is really foreign to anybody that had ridden in the usual English way, so once you get the art of 'dropping your hands', racehorses tend to ease up and stop, well most do!! I freely admit, I have been run off with umpteen times on a gallop and can actually remember one of the funniest (after the fact) occasions. Back in 1996, while we were living in Lambourn, in Berkshire, Bob got offered a job in Dubai as a trainer. It was for a German who owned a small 'string' of horses there and wanted them trained out in the sun in one of the smaller states. It made sense that I would ride out some of the horses as that would be one less member of staff and a job for me too! The problem was, I had no real experience of racehorses apart from once jumping off one at a flat out gallop as I was convinced it was not going to stop before the fast approaching hedge. If you think that sounds brave, it wasn't! It is amazing how fear can give you the strength to count to three, take your feet out of the stirrups, and then launch yourself into midair where you think you have a better chance of survival. This, at the time, seems preferable rather than getting 'splattered' when you have no strength left to help yourself on an unpredictable descent!

So, if I was to ride abroad, I would have to learn fast. We were very naughty, in the afternoons I would tack my little Thoroughbred x Cob mare, Misty, who was only 14.2 hands high, and sneak onto the gallops. Bob, an ex-jockey, was giving me instruction of how to ride short and change my hands and do all the different things. It was brilliant; my little mare went like stink and even faster the other way when we saw the gallop man coming! (A gallop man spends hours on a tractor rolling them to remove the hoof prints, keeping them smooth for racehorses to be exercised on. So, people who sneak on without permission are likely to receive his wrath if caught). We did this a few times until we heard in the pub that the gallop man was asking if anyone knew who owned a little black horse?! Bob knew a great head lad in a small yard and who said he would have a word with the 'Boss' and see what he could organise. Anyone in racing reading this will know that it is a very hard, physical job, which I discovered very quickly. After mucking six boxes out, I was put on my first horse. We trotted along the road and then reached the gallops, I shortened my stirrups, as I had practised, and somehow made it to the top and the mare eventually stopped, but only just! My next horse was called Pow-wow. He was such a cute horse, and had been in several racing yards, but was yet to win a race. We set off up the gallop and he was fine, until the Boss came up-sides (racing term for horses working side by side), and he took off like a bullet! I can still remember that feeling of my backside swinging out of the saddle, as much as I didn't want it to - I had no choice! It was one of those surreal moments, as it seemed like slow motion, in a fast film, as the Boss was beside me trying to give me instructions of how to 'try this' and how to 'do that!' Amazingly, Pow Wow stopped at the end and as I captured my breath, the Boss turned to me and said, "Can you do eight stone? I have never seen that horse shift so fast in his life!!"

"No, definitely not!" was my instant reply. Racing was really not my game, and I used to think at the bottom of the gallops, "Oh, I hope you don't run off with me," and invariably they did!

Funnily enough, when we got to Dubai the contract was not as we had been led to believe. So within six weeks we returned back to the UK, and without me having to sit on a single horse! To get home, we had to help fly four of the British racehorses back home. I say 'help'- we were actually travelling back in a Boeing 747 transport plane, that had enough space inside to fit in two massive Rolls Royce aeroplane engines, and room for these four horses too. Bob and a Racing Lad sat with the horses, which to my surprise, treat flying the same as being in a trailer; they really don't seem to worry. So if you are nervous about your horse being flown somewhere, I have experienced it firsthand and I saw no signs of fear at all. As I said, Bob and the Lad were down with the horses. And me? Well, I was the unofficial air stewardess upstairs in the cockpit! I made the tea, and heated the pilot's food, so without fibbing, I could actually say I have been an 'Air Stewardess', but only for a day!

So back to horses... Don't get me wrong, lots of ex-racehorses make brilliant horses for another career. Most of them have manners and when they are not 'corned up', (fed on oats; which are high in protein, to aid racing speed and stamina) they are not so fired up and can go on to do marvellous second careers.

People like Tiff have to spend a long time to re-educate them to not to lean on the bit, and to work from their hocks. This is so they can go in close to their jumps, unlike a long stride at a racing fence, and generally learn how perform all over again. She had been doing very well with Arnie and had even managed to do three 3-day-events; which to the non-horsey people reading this consists of dressage, show jumping and cross country. Tiff needed help, as on the fourth event, Arnie had acted out of character for him and she wanted to know why.

He was so easy to talk to and came across as sweet natured but rather nervy underneath, and told me if he was bullied, he reacted against it. He showed me him shying at things but nothing bad, and he was very happy with his life with Tiff. She asked me to ask him what happened at his last event. I did, and, hesitantly, he showed me 'slamming his brakes on' which also seemed to be slightly downhill. I asked if he had refused or tried to get out of jumping a jump, and she said I was very near. She explained, "It was the last ditch near the end of the course. He had jumped all the big jumps and ditches but he would not go near this one, and in the end we got eliminated."

She had not given him a hard time for refusing, but at every attempt to get him close, he ran backwards or sideways. I 'put' him back at the ditch and he showed me the ground which looked slippery, and Tiff confirmed that it had rained really hard. He then told me that he was scared as he knew a horse had had a bad fall, and that it and the rider had been slightly injured, so there was no way he was going near! Again, Tiff knew about this accident and said that she totally understood his reason now. She said that having taken him schooling since, he really seemed to lack confidence and, as much as she tried, he just seemed tentative. The problem was; they were entered for a big competition the next weekend, so really needed help, and fast at that!

I explained to him that Tiff quite understood his fear over the ditch and she didn't blame him, but why was he finding it so hard now? He said he knew it was 'silly' but he was finding it difficult not to worry about what he had to do, and what he would face next. I asked him what would help, and he suggested that when Tiff walked the course, that she really took a good mental picture of each and every jump. So, as they went round, as soon as she had jumped one, she could give him the picture of what he would be jumping next. That way he would feel more confident and there would be no 'nasty surprises' – for anyone that takes part in these type of equestrian events, some fences can look rather menacing to the rider, let alone the horses. Tiff agreed that she would do that and mentally pass them on as she rode round. One thing we did have to refuse to agree to, was his request that if he really did not like anything, could he not just go round it? I explained that if he did, he would be eliminated and *not* be allowed to continue. This would be such a shame as he really loved jumping, and to please remember that Tiff would look after him. I wished her luck, and as Arnie had said he would do his best, I felt positive as this sounded willing, and that is half the battle.

That weekend passed and on the Monday Tiff sent me a text saying, "It worked. Thank You!" I was delighted and then she sent me an email saying that her husband, having read my book, would like me to speak to their terrier, Thomas. In the email was an update on Arnie, and how well they had done, and here is an excerpt:

'I took him to Cheltenham and he did all that I asked. I have always shown him the show jumps in that 'picture' way, so to run through the course for the cross-country jumps too, was not any trouble to do the same. It worked! He was such a star and jumped everything, even a horrible ditch at the bottom of a muddy slope at the end of the course, bless him. From then on I have done the same thing at all the events and he has become braver and bolder. The last event he did was Broadway, in October, and he came third! He had a 32 % dressage score, the cross-country was a regional final course, and many horses had trouble with it! We have really strengthened our bond, it is wonderful. Recently I took him to do a competition called Event Training. It involved doing a dressage test, then approx 20 fences which were half show jumping, half cross-country. On the website it looked straight forward, but the course had really tight turns. There was a post and rail fence with trees that formed a sort of tunnel effect on landing side, complete with a sharp turn left to more rails to jump out of the 'tunnel'! There were corners, three hedges with offset rails in them, a water tray with floating ducks, narrow triangle fences (which he had never seen), a big narrow white gate with a curve on the top to finish!! He jumped everything without question. I love him; he tries so hard for me.

When things go wrong you start to wonder if your horse likes his job and you wish that he could tell you what he needs, so naturally your name popped into my head when I was searching for answers.

Thanks so much.

Tiff.'

"Red rosettes are the best, everyone knows that!"
A bumptious pony expressing his knowledge of what competing is all about.

"A bit like an old man with the look of 'do I have to?'"
An elderly pony describing the very expressive faces he pulls to convince his owners he really didn't have to do it, did he? And they worked a treat!!

"Some jiggery-pokery required!"
A rather descriptive way of a horse telling us he wanted a chiropractor!

"So what did I invent then?"
A horse's smart retort when he thought he was being described as an ex-*inventor*! We did explain the actual word was - *eventer*!

Out of Sight

Maelea is a lady who is in her mid thirties with a rather large menagerie of animals and I have had the delight of talking to most of them. Her life is very hectic as she runs a dog-minding service for people that go to work all day. One of the dogs she has looked after for nearly ten years and is affectionately known as her 'Monday to Friday' dog. Maelea's plethora of animals consists of two horses, Pelé and Oki, one dog, Watson (known as Wattie), and his best mate, Gally, her Ragdoll cat. Incidentally, Gally was clearly identified by Wattie with the presentation to me of a picture of a white backside! This is where Wattie likes to shove his nose which, in turn, makes Gally grab Wattie's legs and try to hang on to him! Apart from them, and her daily visitors, she also had a large selection of rabbits and smaller furry species too which she has taken on from a local rescue centre.

Her horses are kept at livery on the same yard as another client of mine, Kerry, and that is how Maelea and I became acquainted. As you might have gathered, I do spend a lot of time laughing and having Maelea as a client certainly enhances that. While trying to solve a small mystery she made me giggle when asking to find out why Oki, her younger horse, had somehow escaped from his stable. She had spoken to me about the fact that the yard was being refurbished and was concerned as her two boys would land up separated. She needn't have worried, they were actually fine. Then early one morning as she had arrived at the livery yard, the owner approached her and said, "I had to tie your horse up last night as somehow he managed to escape. I have no idea how or why, but don't worry, he is okay!" Maelea was slightly confused and not quite sure what he meant so whilst heading over to the stable chatted some more. She got there and found the *door* tied up with string, not the horse, and Oki standing happily with his head over it expecting breakfast! On closer inspection she found he had literally pushed the bolt catches out of the wall and the door had swung freely open. There had been no apparent reason for him being upset, well, not that anyone knew of anyway. What did tickle Maelea however was; having now seen Oki fit and well, was the fact that had he been that upset, she thought the baler string would have hardly held fast considering as he had already removed the permanent fixtures! I was quickly given a picture of him rubbing his backside and actually dropping his weight down against the door for maximum effect. I checked with Maelea if he did this, and she said he did in the summertime but had not seen him do it for months. We concluded that this probably was the cause and it gave us great amusement thinking of this door under pressure then …splat!! No harm done, but I think longer screws would have been required.

Maelea's dog, Wattie, was a two year old Orange (that is technically correct) Roan Spinone (pronounced Spinoney) who Maelea has trained to be a guide dog for herself!! Yes, you read that right, for herself! This is truly unbelievable, but this is absolutely genuine - Maelea is totally blind, having lost her sight to cancer at the tender age of four, and has two glass eyes. On the subject of glass eyes, she gave me a humorous quick run-through of the 'glass eye service'. I had not thought of this fact but as we get older apparently our eyes fade in colour, so, to keep up with reality, every so many years Maelea gets new and slightly less bright ones. She made me laugh with her simplistic description, "Oh, it's really good you know; you go to the eye hospital, they check all the measurements and then you go to the canteen, have some coffee and sandwiches, and within a few hours you have a new pair of eyes!!" She makes very light of her problems, but I know she has countless operations and treatment, but really is not one to complain.

I assure you, when talking to Maelea you would never know she is blind and she talks like she can see and I have got used to that, so I say it as it is, and being highly intuitive , most things she can sense and other things she will get Kerry or someone else to check out for her. In keeping with Maelea's attitude to life and sense of humour, she never declares to newly encountered people that she is blind, as she says, "In the end they get it!" This was borne out when she had advertised for a sharer for her horse. This way she would have help with the bills and Pelé, her twenty-two year old, would get more exercise with another rider too. The girl arrived and Maelea suggested that she would show how well behaved Pelé was by riding him first. She told me that when she 'parked Pelé' as she puts it, at the mounting block, for some reason, unbeknown to her, she thought he was the wrong way round. So, with her still standing on the mounting block, asked him to turn round, which he did by swinging quietly round with

Maelea still holding on to the end of his reins. This must have shown off his lovely manners and obedience to his future sharer who was rather bemused as Maelea mounted Pelé and proceeded across the yard…backwards – well, horse going forwards, but Maelea facing backwards!! But with no panic attached, Pelé started slowly strolling across the yard. Maelea quickly got her reins sorted out and then swung her leg over and twisted herself into the saddle to face the proper way!! But this time the new sharer had been joined by others on the yard who were laughing and quite relaxed about the whole thing. No more demonstrating needed, and the girl still is his sharer nearly a year later, and says that she is so glad to be allowed to share him with Maelea. I bet this relationship has brought something very special into her life too.

I have to say, to most people Maelea would sound unbelievable but this is totally genuine. She is such an inspiration to us all and I am very lucky to have got to know her. The introduction came by chance (if there is such a thing!) really when I was talking to Kerry's horse, Merlin.

Merlin was a seven-year-old, rich mahogany bay and a very striking looking horse. They were having a few issues but nothing major. He had some physical problems which a chiropractor did find and sorted them out for him. He absolutely adored Kerry and described himself as a 'true gentleman' which was totally apt, although he made my work slightly hard as all his answers were in such long sentences, I had to keep doing 're-caps' as my memory is not the best and I do try to repeat, word for word. He made us smile when asked what he thought he was good at, and his reply, "I am excellent at standing still, rather like a sentry really!" and seemed very proud of that fact too!

To the question, "Is there anything you don't like?"

Merlin's answer was, "Horses cutting in front of me!"

I couldn't really work out exactly what he was talking about, as he admitted that his 'brakes' weren't that good when trying to stop him at the end of a canter. I had to ask if this made any sense to Kerry. She said, "I know, it is when we are hacking out, try asking him about the rider," was her cryptic reply. So I did, and all I got was a vision of someone who looked quite animated, as in obvious arm movements, but that was it, so I admitted defeat.

"She is blind," stated Kerry.

"What?" I burbled.

"Yep, she is totally blind!"

"But you were just talking about when you were out riding and cantering," said by me with that questioning tone due to the immense un-believability of it.

"Oh, yeah," Kerry replied in her Kiwi drawl, "she does it all, she is amazing, and I bet after this she will want you to talk to her horses too!" So thanks to Kerry, Maelea did contact me and we have had hours of fun, which have incidentally included me narrating some stories out of my last book to her. She has a very clever computer that speaks to her, but she calls him 'Marvin' (apparently after the depressed robot from the *Hitch Hikers Guide to the Galaxy*!) as he can be a bit temperamental. She says he does tend to narrate at speed, so she has to concentrate to keep up! It is an excellent system she has; as I talk to her animals, she repeats the answer to Marvin and that way she has notes that I am sure are far superior to most of my client's notes!

Whilst talking to the amazing Pelé he gave me a question for me to ask her: "When we are riding in the ménage, how does she know where we are?"

"Great question," I replied, (knowing how 'un-precious Maelea is about her blindness) "I would like to know too!"

"By the wood," Maelea replied.

"Err, I don't understand," I said back, and then she enlightened me to something that I would never have had thought of. Wood has a certain energy (we, and everything, are all a type of energy but I won't cause confusion by going into that) which can be clearly felt by those aware of it. So when you walk in the woods, the trees give out energy thus creating an energy field and one can feel how weak or how strong it is depending how near they are. This amazed me and, even more so, that even if it has been cut down and made into fencing, as in the ménage perimeter, Maelea is totally aware of its energy force. So, the nearer to the fence she is, the stronger the feel and vice versa. This still amazes me, and recently I watched a programme that shows this can also be achieved in a different way. They have taught blind people to 'click', which is a special way of using their tongue to make this noise to 'throw' at their surroundings. By judging the 'return' they know how far the object is, and what type, i.e. solid like a wall, or not so, say like a bush. This all takes highly tuned senses, but when you lose one, the body is so clever, it can enhance others to make up for it.

Going by the mounting (parking) experience, you, I am sure, realised that Pelé was a very special horse, and what beggars belief, Maelea's other horse is a baby in comparison. He is only a four year old, and she is teaching him!! Oki, as he is called, is lively and vibrant, but listened to all that I said and assured me that he knew he had to take care of Maelea. Horses are such incredible creatures; they have this inbuilt intuition and just know when they really have to look after someone. This reminds me (which I am sure Maelea wouldn't mind me sharing in her story) about my lovely little mare, Misty. She was part Thoroughbred, part Welsh Cob, was often referred to as 'Miss Bustle'. She was so busy and everything had to be done yesterday, which, to be honest, gave me years of some dodgy, heart stopping moments, but such fun and enjoyment. Having not ridden for a year because of my cancer, I got it into my head that I had to start riding her again. Although I was still as weak as a kitten and in spite of Bob's reservations and advice (neither of which I listened to!), all I wanted was to take her for a walk down the local bridle path. Misty stood like a rock for me to mount her and somehow I clambered aboard. Bob was doing his best to not look concerned, but most definitely was. He escorted me on foot to the path and I insisted that I would ride so far along and then come back, and that I would be fine. He waited and we set off, at a very slow walk indeed. When I got further along, I was feeling delighted with myself and thought I would venture a bit further, but this meant negotiating a gate. I decided to get off, and thought I would use the gate to get back on once I was the other side. Now, for a horse that would try and push gates open or shut for you (whether or not at that precise time you wanted her to!), Misty, bless her, patiently waited as I heaved (well it felt like that) the gate open, manoeuvred her round it and closed it again. I gathered my breath and climbed up this gate, to nearly the top rung so I could just 'plop' on board. Well, just as I 'plopped', she stepped aside and I just flopped to the floor, with no bodily resistance whatsoever! Misty didn't move a muscle, just looked down with a look of 'What are you doing? But don't worry, in your own time!' This brought tears of frustration to my eyes but I battled back up the gate, repositioned Misty and this time managed to get astride her. I went to the end of the track, came back to the gate, got her through it, and led her back down towards Bob. His face looked aghast, but I smiled, said I was okay, but thought she deserved a pick of grass before he helped me back on her again! I thanked her, and will never forget that, she really knew how weak I was. But, let me tell you; once I was well she was back to her normal forward going self, so much so, that Bob and I in the end swapped over horses, as his Thoroughbred was a quieter ride!

Oki did have one naughty habit though: when people would go past, either just themselves or with their horses, he would poke a back leg out, as if to kick. Although he had never actually kicked anyone, it was causing concern. I had a word with him about it, and found out that it was just childish behaviour so I set about explaining to him that it really had to stop as it was not the done thing. He offered me the bonding key words, "Oki, grow up!" which I thought was very apt and suggested that Maelea use this when she hears someone chastise him for 'lifting a leg'. She said she would go one step further and tell the other girls on the yard the words to use, and she did! And guess what, he was told a couple of times and never did it again!! Maelea was delighted (as was I) and at the same time we found out one thing that was bothering him though. He complained that a light shone brightly into his stable, and it was annoying him. Maelea knew nothing of this and checked with Kerry, who also knew nothing of it either! But within a couple of weeks I got an email telling me that they had gone down late one evening as Kerry had suddenly realised she had left her camera behind. And there, sure enough, was the new security light beaming straight into his stable every time anything set it off!

So onto Wattie, Maelea's guide dog, who was preceded by Adam, who was a yellow Labrador. Adam was happily living out his retirement at the grand old age of fifteen, at her dad's house. I also have chatted to Adam, who described himself as 'gregarious', and was a gem of a dog, as you would expect, and Wattie just loves to visit him and her dad. He told me that when her dad says, "Wattie, Wattie, Wattie," to him, he knows it is because he is so pleased to see him. When asked about the family he told us that her dad was the 'senior trustee' that looked after everyone, and as for his wife (Maelea's step-mum) he could not remember her name, but thought she spent most of her time in the kitchen! Maelea laughed and laughed and said she must tell her, as it was so true. She loves cooking and when they visit she is always baking or preparing something to eat.

How anyone trains their own guide dog, I have no idea! I am sure by this point you are realising that this girl is exceptional and so are her animals. In between Adam and Wattie, she had actually rescued another Spinone, Bos, who sadly died at the tender age of four. When she had rescued Bos she found he was just naturally trying to step into Adams 'shoes', by starting to guide her voluntarily. Because of this amazing dog, Maelea decided to get a Spinone pup and train him up to be her proper guide dog.

Wattie told me that he had been 'given' (as in spiritually) to Maelea as she spends her time giving to others. He also knew he was going to be her guide dog before they ever met! This I can quite believe. So many times I have heard and seen that a certain animal has gone to a certain person, so to me, there is so much that is not out of the realms of possibility. Maelea then told me about her extraordinary dream...She had dreamt one night of an Orange Spinone pup that had an obvious orange spot, centrally placed on top of his head! With that, she was guided to look for a breeder. You can just imagine how that conversation went when she asked if she had one with that unusual description, and this from a girl who is blind! But yes, you've guessed it, she did and he was the only one in the litter like it, and was just at the age ready to be sold. So Wattie was brought into Maelea's life and a huge part of it he has become. There was a 'cross-over' period when Bos was still alive and, according to Wattie, Bos instructed him. One very important thing he impressed upon Wattie was that he must watch out for Maelea - always note where her legs were so as not to trip her up. Maelea was devastated when Bos went to Heaven, but she had played a part in his life, as he had in hers.

It was interesting for me to ask Wattie what it was like to be a guide dog, and he certainly relished his role. He walked with pride as they were such a team. Between Maelea and him they had worked out how to teach each other, which does take huge trust and confidence but she would let him do his bit. Having watched Bos, Wattie had learnt a lot but when he was unsure he would let Maelea take over and show him how to go round an obstacle for example, then he would take her into consideration once he had learned how to do it. One thing that did tickle us was that he complained that people did not park their cars neatly in proper straight lines! This you would think strange from an animal's point of view, but to guide dogs, which are constantly looking for every obstruction, I guess they would notice this, along with everything else. He also let us know that people can be rather ignorant and come too close, thus blocking his view to guide her, but on the whole they were pretty good.

Wattie was brilliant at the yard with the horses and showed me him sitting in front of them waiting patiently, probably taking a well earned rest. There was one thing, however, that Maelea was having a problem with - if she tried to go and tip her wheelbarrow, Wattie would jump up and get extremely frantic as if to try to stop her. I asked him why, and he showed me the pot-holed ground! "Why would that concern you?" I asked him, and he gave me a picture of Maelea pulling a wheelbarrow behind her, and then said she might trip going into one of these pot-holes! I repeated his reasoning, and we thought it was a fair comment and would he have any suggestion for her to make her safe and him able to relax?

"Yes", he replied, "if she was to push it in front of her instead, she would feel a rut or hole through the wheel and know to be careful."

Good logic there we had to agree, and to let him know that she was heeding his advice, she was to say, "It's all right Watson, I am going with my wheel guide!!" That was so funny with his personal choice of words, 'wheel guide'. It does sound very farfetched, but I make nothing up, and this worked a treat! She said it a few times and he just lay there quite unperturbed and still does!

To finish the conversation I asked Wattie what he wanted to say to his extraordinary and wonderful owner, and this is what he said: "She is the most special girl in the world." I, and I think everyone, would most certainly agree with that.

Weighing on her Mind

I have been very fortunate that the television programme on which I appeared on Sky has been repeated a few times, and every time people have contacted me for one reason or another. This lady had watched and said it struck a chord with her and thought she would dearly love me to talk to her horse 'GP'. His owner has chosen the 'anonymity' names, and you will see by the story why they needed to be changed.

Anna has owned GP for several years and really felt they had a special connection and she was not wrong. He introduced himself to me by saying, "I am lovely, I sometimes get a bit 'giddy' (silly) at times but am respectful and good!" I repeated it to Anna, and she agreed that about summed him up.

GP basically took over the conversation and told me what a wonderful body he had and was a very 'correct' mover too. Anna laughed, and said, "Yeah, when he wants to do it!"

To that he replied, "I do, but not again and again." He then proceeded to inform me that he was, 'In no way a nasty horse that would just 'stick his feet in' and do horrible things'. Anna agreed and said that he did try and that she was aware that he found it hard. GP had not always had this beautiful body. When she bought him he was four years old, underweight, under-muscled and been 'tied down' with every riding gadget possible. He was quiet and depressed and when Anna had finished telling me this, he duly informed us that his previous owner 'Didn't give a toss!' Anna totally agreed and said that was exactly her impression and was so glad that she bought him and got him away from there. She immediately removed all his physical restrictions and rode him like a 'free' horse so he could learn to move and balance himself naturally. Within six weeks, he had really perked up and now this cheeky, but loving side had really emerged. The bond had been formed and was to go from strength to strength.

Anna herself is very intuitive and, like me, sometimes when you just 'know' something you just say it. A recent example of mine was whilst my friend, Bronwyn, was giving me acupuncture. As she removed a needle from my foot, I heard, 'That's your liver done then,' and immediately said, "Ah, so you've done my liver then!"

Well, her face was a picture and she said, "Oh my goodness, that *was* your liver point I was working on!" We still laugh about the shock I gave her, but sometimes it can be misconstrued as trying to be a 'smart arse'. Anna said in many situations too, she just said it 'as fact'; like once, when a saddler approached her horse with a saddle to try and the words simply fell out of her mouth, "That won't fit!" This was not because it looked very wrong, it actually turned out to be fairly near but not right, but she 'just knew', and she was correct.

GP got back to telling me about his dressage and said that he was willing, but found it hard. Anna immediately said she knew that and did give him more leeway as he was slightly higher in his backend so she realised that he used more effort than most to engage his quarters. He said that if she could do his warming up for schooling within ten minutes, consisting of walk, trot and canter, this would make work far more interesting. I passed that on and asked if she thought that would be okay and she agreed. Anna pointed out that dressage teachers tend to impress upon their pupils that not until the first gait (walk) is right, then, and only then, can you move onto the next one. This is the same in trot before the horse gets to canter, and cantering is what GP loved to do the most. We set up the agreement that she would try the quick warm up and he also asked if at the end he could have his 'buzz' as a reward? His 'buzz' was to be able to canter around the school in a slightly freer and faster fashion than in his usual dressage style, this was also readily agreed.

I decided to check GP over physically and he immediately offered that his head was 'put on a bit tight!' Now that might sound very strange but actually it makes perfect sense for some horses, and he was one of them. If you run your hand up to the base of your horse's ear and then bring your finger down slightly you will feel a groove. The edges of this groove are made up of the large curve of the back of their lower jaw bone (proper name, the Ramus) which sweeps up to make the back of their head, in effect. The other side of this groove is the wing (edge) of the Atlas bone which is the first vertebra that sits next to the skull. If you can place three fingers in, side by side, that's plenty of width. But, when it gets less (it can even go down to just one finger width) then when you ask these horses to bend for dressage and carry their heads in the 'correct' vertical position, the Ramus is often pushed tightly to the Atlas; in other words, these two bones will meet. This can make a horse's work rather uncomfortable and it may resent keeping its head in that position, so if you are looking for a dressage horse, this is a good thing to check out.

GP kept mentioning to me how good his back was and showed me the good muscle tone, which I repeated each time he did. Anna then asked me if I could ask him if she was too heavy for him. Although that is quite a delicate question for me to ask, I had had no indication of him stopping working for her, so boldly asked him. His reply, "She sits well balanced in the middle of my saddle, and does not sit heavy on the back of a saddle like some do." I repeated this and thought that this would cover whatever weight she was as it was not a problem to him. With that question neatly answered she asked me to check if the radio on the yard bothered him and, with that, he said it was no different to listening to a tractor going round a field! Anna was relieved that it was not upsetting him and admitted that sometimes one of the girls on the yard turns it up a little louder than she would like. With that, he gave me a picture of quite a sturdy looking person and I asked if the perpetrator was quite well built? Anna said she didn't think so and was he referring to her? I said I was sure he wasn't, what size did she reckon the girl was? "Average, probably about a size twelve or fourteen, I suppose."

Something just made me ask, "If you don't mind, what size are you?"

"A ten," came back the reply.

"Pardon?" I queried.

"A ten," she repeated. And then it all flooded out.

Anna was being pushed about by people on the yard and had been told the reason her last horse, who was seventeen hands, had thrown her off, not once but twice, was because she was too fat for him! She freely admitted that then she had been about a size fourteen to sixteen, and I quickly said to her, "You have seen me on TV, and I am a size fourteen!" She said I looked fine and then told me she battles with anorexia. Earlier this year she had at one stage gone down to a size zero and then people on the yard had told her she was too weak to ride! She couldn't win! Anna said she had managed to get up to size ten by the summer and had stayed at that for these past six months and stated that she never wanted to go back down again. I was so incensed that people's thoughtless bullying could reduce someone's life to such a degree. I said that I would like to ask GP for his help on this and give her something to 'hold onto' when things got a bit rough in life. He said, "Beauty comes from within, and that whatever you do to yourself, you will never please them." Then he really got into his stride, saying, "People can be bullies, would you let them bully me?"

"No way!" was her instant reply.

So I said, "That says it all. If you wouldn't let it happen to him, then why would you let it happen to yourself?"

"Good point," Anna agreed. With that, my guide kicked in with some information that I just had to pass on.

When you crash diet and deprive your body of its vital nutrients it can cause the onset of osteoporosis and Anna said she was also well aware of this. Most people think of this condition is one that causes brittle bones and broken legs and such like. I then informed her that a friend of a friend had had this same disease but it had, shockingly, caused her rib cage to collapse and she had died. Anna was taken aback and said how desperate that must have been. I pleaded with her to take all of this on board as I felt that this was so important and this was why this reading had been guided for her to do. After all, there was nothing wrong with her horse and she had got herself away from the bullies but said she was so glad to be reassured by her horse and would remember what he had said.

We ended the call and, although it was not my usual topic of conversation, I felt this was hugely important for her to know and for anyone reading this, please think carefully - You have only one body and you need to care for it, and cherish it, even if it is not 'perfectly sculpted'. I got cancer that was not brought on by my own actions, as neither was the osteoporosis that poor lady had. But, could you imagine having a disease that you maybe feel you brought upon yourself? If this story helps anyone then I am glad to have been of service to you too. I think this story also goes to show that if you don't have anything good to say, maybe it's better to say nothing at all.

I checked with 'Anna' about writing this story and only whilst writing it did I realise that we had missed a valid point. She had recalled about how terribly thin and what poor condition GP was in when she bought him; so the moral here, folks, is if it ain't good enough for them, well it certainly ain't good enough for us!

Rewarding

I absolutely adore the work I do, although some animals can be a lot harder to talk to than most, but they are in the minority. Nearly all owners are superb even if they take a little bit of time to 'get into it' but do, in the end, treat it like talking to their child! I spend so much time laughing and a small percentage crying but I wouldn't swap this work for all the tea in China, as it is what I feel comfortable doing.

As with any job, it is not always fair and just but I count myself very lucky: one, to be alive and two, to get paid to help animals and their owners. If you are one of my clients you will know that I keep my price down as much as I can, as the feedback I ask for from my cases can result in a story I can feature. I get to write these books and in turn live well enough to be happy and do this work that I know is my vocation.

I am very honest and hope that people will be with me. On the one occasion my result saved a horse from going very promptly to Heaven, but I was rather surprised at the result that was in store for me.

I got an email on a Wednesday evening which basically read to the tune of, 'Please help, tomorrow 'Millie' (as I shall call her) is going to be put down, please help!' I had no idea what this girl, 'Yvonne', wanted but thought I should reply and see what I could do. I sensed that this was maybe not her horse so asked her to clarify that also. I was right, she ran a yard, and the horse belonged to a client who gave her consent for the communication. Millie was supposed to be going to be put down the next day but someone had suggested she contacted me first and her client had agreed to this. I said this was obviously a very sad situation but what did she expect me to do? She had followed my standard email, sent the photo and details but had neglected to mention any form of payment but implored me to phone her saying she would explain. I was in a bit of a quandary as to what I was supposed to be doing but decided to call anyway. She didn't beat about the bush - she said the vet was booked but had thought it would be an idea to hear what the mare had to say herself, as I might be able to help change the outcome. I agreed there and then to see what I could do and due to the urgency said I would fit her in when I had completed my evening's bookings.

If you can imagine this, the mare was fully aware of her apparent fate the next day so it was not really straightforward at all. She talked rationally to me and explained that she had had a virus but was feeling better now! I passed this on, and was still not quite aware of why she was supposed to be going to Heaven. She said that she was still lethargic but had been the same for four days now and was better, not worse. This all rang true and Yvonne then volunteered, "But it is because of what the vet found she might as well be put to sleep now." I was so confused and felt in rather deep water and Yvonne was suitably emotional as well. She said she really liked the horse and thought it was sad for this six year old to not be given a chance. I pushed for more answers from Millie and she informed me that her blood was 'all wrong'. Yvonne said that was exactly it, she was not producing white blood cells. The vet said that should she catch an infection she would never be able to fight it off, so it would be easier to let her go now, rather than her suffer at a later date. I asked Yvonne if I was, in fact, 'fighting Millie's corner' for her and she said that the owner was prepared to listen to what came out.

Millie then was quick to show me a picture of her holding up her right front foot and indicated an abscess. I asked if she had had one and the reply came back as "No," followed by a quick, "Yes she did actually, about four months ago."

With that Millie said, "Well, I'm not dead am I, so did I not fight it off then?" We thought this was a valid point especially as they were under the impression that this blood disorder had only been found by chance. There was a distinct possibility that she may have always been like it; who could tell?! It seemed so unfair that she was not even going to be given the chance to see if she could recover should she have a problem in the future.

So, I thought I would clear things up once and for all, and asked Yvonne straight out, "Do you have the power to stop this horse being put down?"

She replied, "Yes, and, in fact, I won't let it happen."

With that out of the way I thought it would be sensible to see if there were any other problems whilst we were there. She was a good riding horse but had been very resistant to go left and showed me her back was very uncomfortable in the saddle area and her pelvis was slightly tilted. Yvonne said she could get the chiropractor to look at her if that would help. The conversation basically ended there, with huge thanks from Yvonne and promises that she would send me the money via Paypal (an internet pay scheme) the next day. Also, most importantly for me, she would let me know how the mare was progressing.

The next evening I got an email from Yvonne thanking me for 'saving Millie's life' and sorry for the delay in payment. This 'delay in payment' story then changed to, "Oh, the owner had just paid me, so I will now pay you."

A week goes by and Yvonne emailed me to say that Millie did have a back problem and now is moving far easier. But guess what - I never did receive payment, unbelievable, eh?! I did manage to suppress my anger but I am only human and just like everyone it is very annoying when you feel someone has cheated you. However, the anger soon dissipated as I realised that the most important thing was that Millie had had her say and that it had helped to extend her life.

I always count my blessings but, sometimes in life, there are situations that are sent to try us. The majority of people that come to me are genuine, however, sometimes I am exposed to those who are not quite so honest, but I do my best to see the positive side even in negative situations and this helps me to continue with my work.

On the odd occasion I have refused payment as I have wanted to 'gift' the reading to someone when I felt it was the right thing to do. One such animal springs to mind; a lovely Greyhound taken in by someone's mother. That someone was actually a nurse whose Collie I had had a chat to when I was having a stay in hospital. Apparently, the nurse's dog definitely improved so she suggested to her mother, Valerie, that she should contact me. The most amazing thing was, Valerie told us that she remembered me and my husband, Bob, as we had met in a shop years before! I must admit she had me flummoxed and I had to ask her for more detail. It was a day in a large, not very expensive, clothing store and we just happened to be looking at fleece waistcoats on a circular rail at the same time as her. We had a very brief chat, as you would to a complete stranger, and apparently I had remarked that they were for Bob. I explained that he was a horse dentist and the green colour would probably disguise the stains incurred by his daily work and that was the extent of the conversation. Little did we know, it turned out she was the mother of a horse client of ours and now many years later I would be helping her with her dog! Again I feel another great example of being 'no such thing as coincidence', just a lovely 'connection'.

Valerie's daughter sent a cheque and picture of a very elderly-looking Greyhound, and rather bedraggled to say the least. This dog had been found early December, totally skin and bone, scavenging around a housing estate. The dog told me he had been loved but they could no longer cope, which seemed strange to us that he should then have been so cruelly abandoned. He then showed me a picture of a building with an obvious neon sign and an arched entrance. Valerie told me it seemed to describe the Greyhound Rescue Centre that was just past the estate. We will never know, and can only hazard a guess - we think they may have dropped him off nearby so they would not have to give any details, hoping within a few hours he would be found and taken to the centre anyway. This obviously didn't happen immediately and he showed me fireworks, and, as any pet owner knows, it is now not a 'one day' thing, they seem to be set off day after day. After talking for ages, it transpired that Valerie had umpteen rescue animals. It came out in conversation that she had just paid a huge vets bill for major surgery on a little spaniel she had rescued less than a month ago.

Valerie is a pensioner and does all that she can, so I told her I would rip up the cheque and to please accept this as my opportunity to be able to give a little back. I felt this Greyhound's life was nearing its end, but at least his last days would be in comfort.

Ringing True

After appearing on the Sky TV show, I had several emails from people who had watched the show. Two lovely ladies, Jan and Neshla even wrote to show to express their appreciation of the content. Jan is from Scotland who helped edit my last book, and is kindly doing with this one too. We have become great friends and she can even make my mistakes seem funny and is a genius at getting me out of my computer mal-functions!

The other lady was from the opposite end of the country, Southampton to be precise. Having watched the programme decided I was probably the person to try to help her dog, Bracken. This dog was approximately eight years old, she had come from a rescue home, and as for her breed, that would be quite a difficult one to pin down. She was quite thick set, a brindle colour and gave me the slight resemblance of a Boxer type head, but without the short nose.

As Neshla, her owner, had watched the programme she knew pretty much how I worked, and so I didn't have to do much explaining. I tuned in with Bracken and what a sweet dog this was. She made such an effort to say how much she loved her family, and was very much part of it. She gave us background information about her previous home - as far as we could gather, she, basically, was just 'in the way' in what seemed a small flat with many comings and goings, and hence landed up in a re-homing centre.

She chatted away but didn't throw any light on an important issue that Neshla thought to be a serious problem. Eventually Neshla asked me to ask her about her barking. I said to Bracken to please tell me about her barking and, with this, she showed me a picture of the impression of a dog wanting to cover its own ears! Strange as that may sound, that is how I interpreted it. She went on to tell me, "I have not always been like this." I told both of these things to her owner and she said she understood on both counts. Yes, the barking had only started a few months ago, and when she barks in the car she does quieten down slightly if her son strokes her ears. We decided that the ear indication may well have been relevant. I pushed on further and asked her if there was a specific problem with her ears, and with that, she gave me the distinct feeling of buzzing - like how I would imagine tinnitus to be. She then let me know that the more noise there was, the worse it got. This again added up, because when Neshla's boys had mates around, she would just start barking incessantly. She also drew me a picture of thickened and narrowed ear canals. My suggestion was to try and steer the vet in the ear direction by describing her reactions to noise in the car and house, in the hope that she would come to the same conclusion about this being hearing related, and check her ears. I thanked her for the chat, and for fun asked Bracken if she had any helpful advice for her owner. She said that there was no need to water the garden every day as plants are a lot hardier than she thinks! This caused a roar of laughter from Neshla, who admitted that she did water most days, as was very proud of her flowerbeds, but would maybe try to cut it down and see what happened. I expressed that I would relinquish all responsibility for any floral demise, and suggested she have a word with Bracken if the case arose!

Within a week, I received an email to say, 'Good news, the vet has found something wrong with Bracken's ears. The canals are smaller than they should be and rather blocked up. I have to put drops in and clean them, she is not amused'. I replied and said that at least we seemed to be getting there and I also had a quick word with Bracken to help the drop regime go more smoothly.

The ear cleaning treatment had been completed and Neshla waited a week or so to see if the barking would stop but, sadly, it didn't. I then urged Neshla to look up tinnitus on the internet so she could casually explain to the vet (who, by this time, was insistent this was not an ear related symptom) to push her to the tinnitus conclusion. Neshla established that tinnitus is related to the nervous system and went back to the vet armed with this information. She was going to ask them if it would be possible to put Bracken on some form of natural treatment for what she perceived might be an underlying nervous condition.

Neshla put her case forward and the vet said, "I wish animals could tell us their problems, it would be so much easier!"

Even with this comment, Neshla was tempted to say, "Why do you think I keep pestering you about her ears?" but was sure the vet would not believe her. Bracken was given a medicine to calm the nervous receptors, so it was then a case of waiting and see what happened.

Great news, an email came through and, yes, it had worked! Bracken had stopped the incessant barking and was so much happier and relaxed. People had even commented on how she seemed to be back to her old self, and the family peace had been restored. This was a brilliant result as, with communication and a lot of perseverance on her owner's behalf, Bracken got her treatment. This is where animal communication comes into a league of its own; Bracken had a condition that nobody could see or hear except herself. Through a stroke of good fortune (or divine intervention, if you ask me) her owner saw me on TV and was then able to set up a chat for Bracken to let me 'hear' all about it.

(I sent the above story for Neshla to read, and her reply warranted a mention too. She thanked me for the way I had written the story, but also to let me know what amused her, and in turn amused me. Quote: "The thing I found amusing is that the other lady who contacted you is an editor – as am I! I too met another spiritual lady who was writing her first book and offered to edit it for her. I did and it has now been published. What a small world!!

"I'd like to be named Mary the Conqueror!"
A clever answer from a three yr old horse, who has found things difficult, but determined to overcome them.

"I think I am getting a bit long in the tooth for all this!"
Yes, this was a horse! He had been competing since he was four years old, and now reached the grand old age of … eleven! Not quite retiring age his owner thought! Bless him, it was worth a try.

"Elegant, with a splash of excitement about it."
A grand, but very accurate from a horse when asked to describe himself.

"It is lovely, but the sheep smell!"
An honest answer from a horse when asked what he thought of his surroundings. Not quite the answer I think the owner was looking for!

Red for Danger

When I start talking to an animal I am aware that they can be 'putting on a front' and, as confident as they may come across, sometimes this is not the case at all. Tara's picture showed me a big, black, medium-built mare with one of those lovely old-fashioned heads. Her owner, Lisa, had come to me as Tara's behaviour was 'rather disconcerting', as she told me further into the reading.

Tara instantly made me feel on edge and gave me the impression you would never know quite what was going to happen next. She would be one I would describe as 'stampy' as she really felt angry/disillusioned underneath so was coming across as bolshie but sorry with it. Yet, surprisingly, she would say sweet things like, "I like children sitting on me, I like the responsibility as it feels motherly!" And also she showed me her taking carrots out of Lisa's mouth, which was so gentle compared to the way she often acted and how she was coming across to me. We were quick to realise that these were things with no pressure attached. If, however, you did have a go at her (her personal description of when Lisa was riding her and putting her 'leg on' to gain impulsion) or generally pushing her work-wise, this had a really adverse effect. This went from not being able to do a dressage movement to knocking down a show jumping pole, anything that caused her to get frustrated.

People were generally under the opinion that she was a 'cow' and this was compounded by the fact that she was a 'kicker' of other horses. Anyone that owns a horse like this knows you have to be so cautious as do others with their horses around you. She spoke to me with such an angst-filled tone but with anger mixed in and then showed me how reactive she was; if she was asked to do something she didn't understand, or tried and got it wrong, when asked to try again she would simply throw herself about and 'rodeo' for England! This was where the word 'disconcerting' came in, which was far removed from what most people would have thought - me included. Fortunately, her owner, Lisa, could see the mare's goodness in spite of all the behaviour issues and was obviously a very brave rider who did not want to give up on her.

We went through all the various difficulties and found out that Tara wanted to please but as soon as things 'fell apart' in her mind, she would just lose it and act accordingly. Lisa was trying to teach her to 'leg yield', which entails getting a horse to go sideways crossing its legs. This may sound strange, but this lateral movement helps 'open' a horse's shoulder and makes them more supple. On people, I guess the equivalent would be when you stretch up your arms and use one arm to pull the other across the top of your head, so you can really feel the 'pull' in your shoulder joint. In the past, when I have been teaching or just simply chatting to dental clients on yards people have complained that a horse goes one way and not the other, saying they thought it was behavioural. I would say, as politely as I could muster, "They don't tend to wake up one morning and say, 'I don't like going right anymore'. There is always a reason for it, whether physical or mental." My comments sometimes went down like a lead balloon, but I always speak up for the animals in the hope that people might give them the benefit of the doubt. Often people would then ask my advice and then the cause would be looked for, and the reasons why. I too have learned so much by listening to others willing to speak up. These can range from tooth trouble, back problems, ill fitting saddles or even riding-based. In this case, Tara would go to the left, but although she was showing willing, she was struggling going right, so I asked her to show me why and what was the difference? It became apparent that Lisa was, for some reason, tilting her right pelvis down, and this was actually blocking her horse's movement. Apparently to get a horse to go to the right, you would not want the pressure above like that; it comes from the opposing leg and hip to get the horse to move away from it. To be honest my dressage knowledge is quite limited but this does seem logical. Now most horses would maybe get a bit 'narky' if you kept trying but when Tara couldn't do it, she would just simply explode. Unfortunately it was very hard for anyone on the ground to see where the riding fault lay, let alone Lisa being able to try and 'feel' it. In spite of all of this, I agreed with Lisa that this mare was not trying to be bad, she just came across as resentful and awkward, and so we would try to find out why.

Before I could ask for Tara's reasons, Lisa suggested maybe I could ask her why she kicks other horses. Tara heard the question and immediately showed me a horse mounting her from behind She then explained that when she was young a colt had 'jumped' on her and, as she objected somehow their legs got tangled and he landed up cutting her down the inside of her leg. Although the previous owners treated it, she was so upset because they didn't seem bothered about it and just put her back out with him! She was simply just expected to put up with it, so hence she became defensive to other horses and gained 'attitude'. We could see her point, and felt that she was only being resistant as she had felt bullied and that her feelings had not been considered. I was quick to remind her that that was in her past and would never happen again as Lisa only wanted the best for her. Tara informed us that there was a mare on the yard that was quite 'mare-ish' (hormonal) and Tara felt that she got others to gang up on her. There had been a real 'set to' as two mares had escaped into *her* field but she said that she kicked out in defence and, actually, it turned out that Tara was the only one that got injured! Lisa said to ask her about kicking Lilly as that really did cause an upset. Suddenly Tara 'withdrew' from me and I really had to push to get her to acknowledge what had gone on. I struggled to get her to talk about it and suggested that if she told me, then I could at least give her side of it. She relented and told me that she felt Lilly was trying to take Lisa away from her! I asked Lisa if she had been asked to ride this Lilly or was looking after her. This was not quite the case. It turned out that the stable next to Tara was used as the feed and store room and that Lilly was stabled on the other side of it. So, every time Lisa came out with a treat for Tara, she would, out of kindness, give one to Lilly too. Tara was so jealous and this had made her feel more insecure so, unfortunately, at a given opportunity, she laid into Lilly and did actually injure her. From that point on, Lisa made a conscious effort to just give Tara the treats, and told Lilly, sorry, but she would have to get hers from her owner.

Tara then volunteered that people used to say nice things about her but now say nothing! This made total sense as, at first, people would comment on how stunning she was, and then talked about the negative issues, especially after the kicking of Lilly. Tara lived in a paddock on her own, so other horse owners did not have anything to do with her. We asked Tara if she was okay with being on her own and she said that she could see the other horses but actually felt safer. We also had a chat about the fact that when she is out in company that Lisa needed to keep her in behind which was not to

Tara's liking as she did want to go faster. The problem was if she overtook and then a horse came close up behind her, in spite of the warning red ribbon in her tail, often the rider would not be able to get their horse out of her way quick enough. Lisa was obviously worried that the horse or even them, themselves would get kicked. We chatted about the fact that although a red ribbon in a tail is a well known sign for 'danger - this horse kicks', yet people still don't pay attention. They land up far too close, and then get annoyed when the horse goes to kick out at theirs!

Having been able to tell her side of the story I hoped that Tara would maybe realise that Lisa was really struggling with her 'over-reactive' behaviour. Lisa at least now felt I had confirmed what she had thought all along. This mare wasn't malicious, just totally insecure. I checked her over physically and there were a few issues but we assured Tara that Lisa would get them checked out.

One thing that did crop up, which often does, was the fact that the hay was making her cough as the spores were affecting her lungs. This is a very common problem and if not addressed you can land up with a horse with COPD (chronic obstructive pulmonary disease) which affects their breathing. The worse scenario being that it can cause your horse to be 'broken winded', which is when they cannot get their breath and show a 'heave line' down their side when trying to get air into their lungs. Unfortunately hay does have spores (and often hay is not of the best standard nowadays with the lack of proper sunny summers) so people soak it and hang it up in a haynet. This is all well and good, but, as it drains over the hours, the top then quite quickly is back to dry hay, so therefore you still have the same problem, although maybe reduced. My own mare, Misty, was a COPD horse thanks to a batch of mouldy bedding straw. One of our clients gave us a great tip - Get a big sturdy plastic tub, put your wads of hay in it and fill with water. Soak for a little while (when it is wet, it is wet!) and then tip the tub over and let the water drain off. Tip it back over and put in the stable. You then have no dripped water on the floor, and the hay stays damp all night. Most horses are great about eating out of this but some are mischievous and will tip it over, so you might need to secure it into an area so they cannot traipse their hay into their bed!! Well worth a try, it worked for us for years, and is actually far easier than filling haynets etc.

I hoped through this chat that I had done enough to convince Tara that Lisa now understood her and she would make sure that no horses were a threat to her either. Tara responded to that positive thought and asked Lisa to say, "You relax and I will watch them for you." I wished them both the best of luck and Lisa assured me that she would follow everything and then come back to me to see how the mare was feeling and how they were doing in general.

On the next chat Tara came across as slightly more relaxed and told me that she realised that Lisa would not let anything happen to her, but then apologised as she had reared the day before! She quickly tried to re-assure me saying, as she put it: 'it was in a controlled way and I was not my normal crabby self after it!' The mare said it was due to the flies, saying they had been a 'nightmare'. Lisa laughed and said that was true, but would prefer if she would stop doing it, whatever, but had noticed that she was subservient afterwards, so maybe one day, just maybe…Tara said that she really felt the pressure was off, and that her bond with Lisa was so much stronger. Lisa agreed and said that things were going much better. Since working her more, there were a few physical issues but nothing major, but having muscled up, her saddle needed to be checked as it seemed to be going off to the right. She was leg yielding well both ways now, and asked if Lisa could still do the in-hand flexibility exercises that she had been shown how to do, as they were really helping. She was also jumping far better and had been doing her dressage schooling with much less fight and drama.

Lisa and many of the other people from the yard had now moved to a new one and I had to laugh at Tara's answer when asked what she thought of the new yard. It was nothing like, 'Oh, the stables are nice', or 'my paddock is bigger', no, it was, "It is better because the muck heap is not so intrusive!" I had to get that one clarified. It turned out to be was that at the old yard they had to walk past it every day, but on the new yard, it was better sited out of the way If it was important to her, then we were pleased for her!

I have to say, this case was tricky and there was no way Tara was going to totally change character. We have to remember animals are individuals just as we people are so I, nor anyone, can change their real personality. Anyway, this is not what Lisa was looking for; she just wanted to understand her horse and maybe come to some compromises if at all possible. In the wrong hands I doubt we would have seen much of a change in her, as Tara has required great patience and a good deal of horsemanship which, fortunately for her, Lisa has in abundance.

Tara tells us that she is still 'stuffy' but is getting 'less stuffy' and Lisa says there are only the occasional 'explosions' but on the whole she is doing very well. In fact, Tara is delighted that people are talking about her again, but this time for the right reasons. She had even been out competing and had actually won some rosettes!

In Lisa's words to me:

"I feel we have come a long way and some people who have not seen her under saddle for a while can't believe the difference in her. They have asked if I've swapped horses! She is listening to me and doesn't kick off (very often) when she doesn't understand or if we knock a jump pole down. I chat to her all the time and she communicates back especially when she wants to be scratched!

I'm trying to remember to have 'team chats' with her the day before we compete and on the day. What amuses me the most is - If she has been a bit moody and I ask her why, she won't look at me! If I'm chatting normally to her, say, asking her to move over in her stable or just general chit chatting and I do the same, she will maintain eye contact! Glad that she is still my 'teenager with attitude!' Her show name is Black Witch and with the red in her tail I'm hoping other riders get the message!"

Back Together

My work can be heart wrenching but nothing could have prepared me, or anyone, for what I was about to hear. I have embellished nothing, but altered the names to ones that 'Fiona' suggested, and certain facts to give anonymity to such a sensitive case. This was back in 2008 and I had received an email asking for help with Fiona's horse, Jenny. She had heard of me because I had helped with some horses in the same area of Scotland as her.

As I explained how this worked, I received simple 'Aye, okays' so I had no idea of what was to occur. I tuned in with Jenny who was a dark bay mare and who turned out to be a Thoroughbred.

"I am not evil," was the first line I was greeted with from a very distressed horse. "Why me? I'm not bad!" she ranted. "It's not fair, I'm not bad!"

Well, she had ranted and ranted, and everything I kept repeating Fiona would say, "Yeah, I know", or words to that effect. I was given visions of this horse rearing and flailing her legs, and again this was immediately recognised. I began to think, if the owner knows she is this upset, what is going on and how is this happening?

I tried to calm Jenny by telling her I was here to help her and, with that, she threw me the saddest line I think I will ever hear, "I'm broken, you won't fix me." With that, I stopped and Fiona offered to let me know what was going on as, by now, Fiona was in floods of tears.

On the night of the Summer Solstice (the first day of summer) this innocent little horse had been out in the field with a group of horses. Some evil, wicked, gutless person/people had managed to catch her, and slash both her back legs with a knife. This heinous human cut her so severely below both her hocks that she was immobilised by the injury and sheer shock. Poor Fiona went into utter shock too when she found Jenny, still alive but in desperate need of veterinary help. Everybody came to the rescue, and somehow they managed to get her back to the yard. Once in the stable, the vet was able to treat her and fortunately her wounds be able to be stitched up.

Having heard all this, I 'pulled myself together' and said that I felt no pain, but all I was getting were these emotional outbursts.

There appeared to be no apparent discomfort, as this had happened many months prior to this call. I pressed on and got the words with the rearing picture, to the effect of, 'No, get off me, don't touch me'. Fiona said that this was the problem, emotionally she was on a different level - Jenny had spent months standing at the back of this stable, and if she tried to lead her out, the mare simply got hysterical and lashed out.

We talked and talked and eventually got Jenny to listen. I explained to her that this was not personal to her, because she was evil or horrible or suchlike. No, it was done by some malicious bully, in the dead of night, who she had trusted to let near her in the field. She had done absolutely nothing wrong, nothing to bring this upon herself, just sadly, we live in a world where evil lurk, but it is very, very uncommon. I assured her that nobody would ever get near her again to hurt her.

As an adult reading this I am sure you are totally appalled, so can you now try to imagine how you would console a child in a situation like this? Well, on top of everything, Fiona's daughter, Emily, was totally hysterical about what had happened to the horse that was as much hers as her mum's.

After about half an hour, Jenny had calmed and was actually chatting away to us about her prowess as a jumping horse as well as being a safe hack for Fiona. Her actual physical injuries still didn't get a mention but she gave us the usual odd bits and showed me that her right pelvis seemed slightly dropped, but nothing significant.

As the conversation got to the end, Fiona happened to mention that the police and newspapers had got involved, due to the public interest in such a heinous crime. Some wanted to link it to a 'cultish' behaviour, as the date had coincided with the Summer Solstice, but most journalists reported it as probably just simply an act of someone deranged.

We eventually finished the call, and I did some emotional healing afterwards just like I had done for the little rescue pony who didn't know where her son was in the earlier story.

The next morning my phone 'beeped' with a text from a number I did not recognise. I opened it and read, 'I can't believe it, Jenny had her head over the stable door this morning, and I am so excited!' This was a huge step forward, if we could achieve this after so many months of grievance, I really felt we had a chance to get her over this. Within a month, we spoke again, and Jenny had really turned a corner, so much so that Fiona had considered bringing her back into work. She, sensibly, called the vet to give Jenny the once over, and although her back legs were healed fine, the vet was rather more worried about her hindquarter action. He said that she looked un-level, and maybe it would be best to retire her and have her like a family pet! What a huge blow -to have got this far then to have all sense of normality returning dashed. I asked Jenny to give me any pain she felt (again nothing) and to give us her opinion about her action behind. She was straight in there with, "I have been like this for years, and I have been ridden and jumped, haven't I? I am no different from then, please let me work!!" We thought logically about this and actually it made perfect sense, but we could see where the vet was coming from, as the injuries had 'highlighted' her backend. Had it not been for that, none of us would be any the wiser as to her not-so-perfect action!

Months and months passed, and I heard nothing, no emails, nothing. I must admit that I did find this hard as a lot of my emotions were still invested in this horse. Although, nowadays, people who book me agree to give me updates, this actually was not a case of not caring or wanting to; the hand of gloom had hit Fiona once again. Don't panic readers - it was not Jenny again, but Fiona herself.

Fiona emailed and booked an update communication to see how things were going. I tuned in and was met with the words, "I am back to my normal self!" Well, from a horse that had been so traumatised, I felt this was a very bold statement and passed it over rather tentatively, in case I had misunderstood or Jenny was putting on a brave front.

"True," Fiona announced, "she is totally back to her same loving self!"

But then Jenny gave me the question, "Why won't *she* ride me then?"

'Ah', I thought, 'has Fiona lost her nerve through all of this, or maybe something else has gone wrong?'

"I can't," replied a very tearful Fiona.

I launched into an, "It's okay, she says she's back to normal, please believe her, she obviously wants to be ridden."

"It's not her, it's me," cried Fiona. She then went on to tell me the terrible news that Fiona herself was ill and in the process of having radiotherapy for cancer of her pelvis.

I was flabbergasted at such bad luck. This was just too cruel but Jenny was again straight in with her 'ten penneth worth', "She's done way better than the consultants thought she would, she is doing really well!" Yet another bold statement from Jenny! Fiona confirmed this and explained that they thought she was making a superb and fast recovery. Jenny wanted to let us know that she was aware of what was wrong with her owner by chipping in with, "And she had felt a strange drilling sensation in her hip, but ignored it!" True again, and we thanked her for her huge knowledge and were sure the consultants would be impressed, should they ever be told of it! (Please note: I act with extreme caution when passing over such personal and sensitive information. But as I have said before, I am only given it if it is right to talk about.)

Now I knew why Fiona wouldn't ride her and, although she thought she could physically do it, was petrified that Jenny would move at an inappropriate moment whilst being mounted. The fear of falling was huge, and completely understandable. I asked Jenny what she could do to convince Fiona that she would not move and that she could be mounted safely. She gave us the assurance that she would stand rock solid and, to prove this, take her to the mounting block and she would stand still for however long it took. Even if she doesn't get on her that day, keep doing it and she will prove it to her. I wished Fiona and her family all the best.

Before I finished, Fiona asked if I had a message from Jenny for her daughter, Emily. I knew that Emily had been crushed by what had happened and was getting pushed around at school. I asked this wonderful horse what she thought could help her and this was what she told us: "People stand on others just to make themselves seem taller!" I explained to Emily what it meant, and I really do think that sums up bullies, big and small to a tee.

On giving Jenny the last word before I finished, as I do with all readings, I was given the dubious task of passing this one on: "I think they should get married!!" Well, talk about putting me in a difficult situation, I know we live in a more modern era, and knowing she had a daughter I went carefully 'round the houses'!

I stuttered, "I am right in thinking you're not married?"

"No, we're not," came back a quick reply, "but we are getting married, later this year in fact!!"

"Oh, well done, you," I chimed, "but could you please tell Jenny as she seems to think it's her job to make sure you do!"

Within two weeks I had an email come through with the subject title in block capitals, "Wayhay, I have ridden Jenny!!!!" I was ecstatic, to say the least, as this had been such a triumph over adversity. I wished them all the best and every bit of luck in the world, they truly had earned it.

Fiona and I still keep in touch and all is well with her and Jenny. This whole episode has had a line drawn under it and is now just a distant memory. Jenny is totally happy, relaxed and back jumping as well as she did before, much to Emily's delight. Fiona did get married later that year (with Jenny's nod of approval, I'm sure, having thought it was her suggestion in the first place!) and as for Fiona - she was able to glide down the aisle without the slightest sign of lameness herself!

As harrowing as a story this has been I truly think it shows how magnificent animals are. Jenny could have been 'broken' forever but she was willing to try and somehow has had the strength to overcome such an ordeal. I have often spoken about this case when I have done talks or demonstrations, as I hope that her example shows what can be achieved with love and understanding, and how well animal communication can work. Every negative has a positive; if Jenny's story inspires someone to get help for their animal by trying an alternative way and, if it gets results then at least some good has come out of it.

Coming and Going

It was the middle of the day and I got an email through from an owner saying that a chiropractor had been on the yard and had suggested that she try me, and it was very, very urgent. I emailed straight back, we got everything organised within the hour, and then I called her.

She was in tears and, to be honest, it was quite a difficult conversation to hold as I didn't know what she was expecting but, between the tears, she sounded rather annoyed! I explained that her horse, Hugo, could also hear what we were saying, which caused a bit of confusion as she was worried because she was not at the yard. I explained that it was immaterial as I work to the subconscious so you do not need to be near them, and also they can be doing as they please at the same time too.

Hugo was a beautiful grey horse and was about twelve years old. He was happy to chat and said that he was genuine and, with that, his owner interrupted with, "Well, that might be his opinion!" I quickly reminded her we were in a three-way conversation and shall I just see what he says? She reluctantly agreed, so I proceeded. He told me what a good ride he was; in fact he was extremely reliable and tried his best for his riders. I put this to her and she agreed, so my mind began to think maybe we are talking 'physical'; after all, it was a chiropractor that had passed my details on. I suggested that I 'body-scan' him, which I do by working from the mouth and all the way back. Some animals just 'stand quietly' as I point out what I can see, whereas others interrupt me all the way through and even ask me to scratch their belly, or tell me not to look 'under there'! This does sound impossible, as does a lot of what I do, but if I can clearly see a picture in my mind, then why can't I try to zoom in and study it closer? I went over this lad and, to be honest, there was really nothing to be found and told the owner that I wasn't being shown any problems. She said that made sense as the chiropractor had been on the yard to treat another horse, but had quickly checked Hugo to eliminate any pain issues. She had found nothing so then had suggested me.

I was getting nowhere, and she was still upset, so I decided to cut to the chase as she was clearly not enjoying this, and neither was I.

I seemed to have a horse that was a good ride and physically sound and that chatted to me like a happy horse, so I decided to put it to her straight:

"What direction do you want me to go in?"

With that she hastily said, "Ask him what he has done to me!"

"Okay," I said a bit hesitantly, and did just that.

"Err, nothing," was his seemingly innocent reply.

"Yes he did! He bit me, ask him why?"

"Oh, that! I didn't mean to," said Hugo.

"Well, it didn't seem like that to me. He has bitten me on my stomach and this is not the first time either!"

I could now see why she was upset and anxious; I would have been the same. If anyone else has experienced a serious horse bite you will know how painful and upsetting this can be. I told her I now understood her anger, however the horse didn't come across as the aggressive type but I would try to find out why.

He showed me someone putting their hand up to his mouth as his head was over the stable door, and as soon as I told her, I got, "That was it; that was the last time he did it!"

"Were you trying to give him a titbit or something over the door?" I asked.

"No," she replied, "I was trying to take his headcollar off."

"Okay," I said, "but do you ever feed him titbits at the door?"

"Very occasionally, but not often as he is a bit of a greedy horse." I now had an inkling what was behind this, so decided to move on and ask about this latest misdemeanour. He then showed me a very calm picture of someone gathering up loose hay from the corner where his food manger was and bringing it across the stable to make a neat pile. I asked her if that picture made any sense and she said, "Yes, it was as I was moving the hay he grabbed my stomach."

So I asked him, "Why did you bite her?"

"I didn't mean to," Hugo replied, "I just thought she was going to take it away again!"

I asked her if sometimes whilst he was eating his food, did they take hay away from his stable? Yes and no was the answer. They would bring new hay into the stable, but if the pile of hay collected was big enough, sometimes they would then take some of the new hay back out of the stable with them. Now this was making sense. Imagine if your favourite food was chips, and someone everyday would bring you your plate of chips, then for whatever reason, remove some of them again on the way out, whilst you were finishing your starter. That would seem rather unfair, after all, you had been looking forward to those chips, and if you were greedy, like Hugo, you probably would have got rather annoyed at trying to eat one course whilst defending your second.

This turned out to be exactly what they were doing, and just as she stood up with the arm full of hay, he lunged to grab some and got her stomach instead. To be honest, no horse should snatch or bite, but unfortunately some do. This often stems from being a youngster when being bolder often meant you got more, very similar to being in the wild. He assured us that he had not meant to do it on either occasion and was extremely sorry indeed, and I truly thought he meant it.

Now we knew, I suggested that she never tries to take his headcollar off over the door so he cannot mistake her fingers on the way up. As for feed times, make sure that his feed is in his manger, the hay is cleared and piled to the right amount, and then put him in the stable and leave him to eat in peace.

By the end of the call, she was much calmer as the shock had worn off and the logic of the situation had taken over. She agreed that she now understood what the problem was, and that he had *not* been 'attacking her'; he was just being covetous of his food. She thought she would be able to cope with him now she had heard his side of the story, although she did admit, however, that she would struggle to trust him for a while. She said he was such a star in every other way and that she had felt in her own heart he wasn't really nasty but was upset nevertheless. At least she knew now it was an unfortunate chink in his otherwise pretty perfect armour.

I didn't get an update personally from this owner, but about six months later, another person booked me from the same yard and assured me that there had been no more incidents and that Hugo's owner had 'got over it' and things were back to normal.

A Wee Mac

The photo arrived, courtesy of Angela, Alex's daughter, of Mac, an aged West Highland Terrier. In his picture, he was staring up at the camera with a real 'look at me' expression across his face. His little eyes were clouded with obvious cataracts but beautiful, nevertheless.

Angela, whose horse I had chatted to, realised that Mac was getting on in years, fifteen in fact, and that it would be so special for her father to have a chat with him before Mac passed to another world.

I remember the call clearly - It was springtime, and I was out on a call with my husband and realised that I was not going to be able to get home back in time So, with the sun streaming through the car window and mobile in hand, I dialled his number.

With a lilting Scottish accent, Alex, a man of quite mature years, shall we say, simply 'fell' into the conversation like he had done it every day! We chatted away and Mac was having such a laugh. He took complete command of the conversation and reminded Alex of what a 'wee bugger' he had been in his younger days. He was just so adored and admitted to purposely making himself centre of attention, at every opportune moment.

Mac was having repeated stomach problems and I confirmed that they were back again and he really did want to see the vet. Mac then informed us how much the vets liked him! He was remembered due to an odd incident, which led neatly to a very old, but unanswered question: The needle that was found inside Mac's tummy: who left it out for him to find and idiotically swallow? "Oh dear," I thought, but quickly established that if the truth be known there would be no repercussions, so the question was put forth. I was instantly shown a cardigan/jumper hanging limply on the arm of a chair, which looked like part of a three-piece-suite.

On passing this over to Alex and asking if there was any recollection, he chortled and said, "I knew it was my other daughter, Susan, she was mending her cardigan and I thought so but was never sure!" Susan had been long forgiven and, I am sure very grateful to her sister for arranging this chat! That incident actually had no bearing on his latter day stomach problems anyway.

As animals do, they often like to tell me how special their owners are and offer reasons as to why they think they are in someone's life. Alex is a very caring man and he looks after his disabled wife. Mac knows that is it very hard work, although Alex doesn't mind in the slightest, but Mac loves to be his distraction and shares the few breaks throughout the day for his little walks. Neither of them goes terribly far but share the same sense of purpose and companionship.

I absolutely loved doing this chat; many people are sceptical and, not being unkind, I generally find the 'older generation' seem to struggle with the concept slightly more. But Alex was an absolute star, and Mac had a field day!

When Mac did eventually run out of things to say, I asked Alex if he had any questions for him and he put this to me, "Why, does he sometimes look like he is looking right past me, instead of at me, when I am talking to him?"

'Mmm, interesting one', I thought so I asked Mac to show me what he did. Sure enough, he most certainly did look past him, because he was looking at something behind Alex!

I looked carefully at the picture that Mac was showing me and first, it was of a hearing aid!! Then, a picture of a man with a hearing aid!! Now we had a picture, complete with sound effects, of a hearing aid whistling!! So, with all that, I gently asked Alex if he knew anyone that used to wear a hearing aid. Straightaway he replied, "Oh yes, my father did, he wore one for years."

With that, Mac piped up, "Well I am surprised the batteries haven't run out!" We both dissolved into fits of laugher and if anyone had been passing my parked car they would have thought me mighty strange!

This wonderful animated vision, given for such a lovely recipient, complete with a classical rhetorical remark. This was actually explained to us that Alex's father is 'up there' watching over him and his wife. At least Alex now knew that when little Mac went to Heaven that his 'grandfather' will be waiting to welcome him to his next 'home'.

"I think he left his brains in a biscuit tin!!"
An apt description from one very sensible Labrador about her younger and not so sensible buddy.

"Cool as a cucumber in the face of adversity."
A horse expressing his very mature and unshakeable demeanour.

"It is all about picnics and parades."
A horse's description of a Point-to-Point.

"Why do they stroke me like they are washing a window?"
A gentle question from a horse at a therapy centre for people. If you think about it, horse people naturally stroke in one direction, but to those who have never encountered a horse, a circular touch would not seem unusual.

War and Peace

My chat with Shep, a black and white Collie (no surprise there!), was actually in a call to Mozambique, Africa. Carrie, his owner, had been passed my name through her sister, whose dog I had recently chatted to, who lives here in the UK.

Shep was four years old, and a very sweet and gentle lad, but physically looked slightly 'odd' to me. It seemed his legs were not straight and strong looking as you would expect with a collie, and when I carefully mentioned this to her, she said she knew what I was referring to. I then heard the word, 'Ricketts', which is such an old fashioned term it took me by surprise as I have never experienced it with veterinary nursing over here. I gave the word to Carrie, and she confirmed that he did indeed have Ricketts. Shep had been a stray which they had rescued, and unfortunately like many dogs over there, had survived on what poor diet they could find or got given. Sadly, as his bones were forming and growing, due to the lack of calcium they did not have the strength and density to be straight and strong. In spite of this, he was still able to lead a full and happy life with Carrie and her husband. (Ricketts used to be fairly prevalent early last century and many people had bowed legs, until the link was discovered that a calcium deficient diet was the cause). Shep, at this point, was not in any discomfort but Carrie was aware that most likely there would be problems later on so she would keep a close eye on him.

Shep was so appreciative of his good home, and was a loving and faithful pet to them. There was one thing though, they could not fathom out and wondered if I could try to.

I quickly established that Shep had a problem about leaving the bedroom, yet he was happy to enter in there!?! Sure enough, he was happy to go and spend time in the bedroom yet got very agitated and barked with some ferocity as he went back to the doorway to try and leave. This seemed to be more at a night-time and I asked if he could show me why, and let me know why now I was feeling so anxious too. Without hesitation, he passed on some very disturbing pictures of people being physically dragged from the room. These were adults and children alike, and the visions were coupled with knives flashing and the sound of screaming. It was so graphically clear, it was like a replay from one of these films where people are taken from their homes and brutally killed for being of a certain colour, culture or creed. I was at quite a loss as to what to say, or how even to broach the subject. Sometimes I really do have to think fast, as the last thing I want to do is alarm someone, so I trod carefully. I decided to ask Carrie if she knew of any history relating to the property that would be anything to do with conflict. She immediately said that the area had been subject to atrocities, so then I was able to freely tell her what I was being 'shown'. Carrie said it didn't surprise her as she had felt 'unrest' in the house too. As people, we can pick up on cold spots, these are eerie areas in a place that have an unhappy spirit that feels trapped and can't move on, often due to the circumstances of their passing. Animals are far more 'open' and can often see things we cannot. It is something to be aware of if you have an animal that is behaving oddly, especially in a certain area of a house, garden etc. If so, maybe think about getting it checked out. I felt sure that this house was holding many sad souls and recommended that she 'smudged' the house throughout. One common way of 'smudging' is achieved by burning dried sage, and wafting its smoke around every wall and corner of a property's rooms to purify and help move spirits on. I have no idea why, or how, this works, but if you talk to people that do this as a job (paranormal work) they understand the 'ins and outs' of it and it often has the desired effect. Carrie said she was more than happy to do this, and I suggested she ask the spirits to leave and go and join their loved ones who have left this earth already as there is no reason for them to stay here in her house now.

I have to say, I found the vision in that reading almost surreal in its clarity. Quite a while later, Carrie and I had a catch up. I was delighted to hear that she had taken advice and 'cleared' her house and from that day Shep has shown no sign of fear around the bedroom door again! An incredible experience for me, and I would say for Carrie too. Although I strive to see with more and more clarity, there are some things in life I would wish that I did not have to witness, even if it is sometimes decades after their occurrence. My work is so variable and things like this are very rare comparatively and at least we got the answers and results that we had both hoped for.

Simply Precious

When I got a call from a large stud farm, the manager, 'Rose', she started telling me about a youngster they had. She was a two year old filly that they really didn't know what to do with. I quickly managed to stop her flow of words as I did not want it to influence the reading which I presumed they were asking to book. This little filly was younger than most I deal with, so I told her the usual low-down, the various options of how to send a photo etc.

Later that day, I received a photo of this bay filly; we shall name 'Sophie' for this story, as to remove her and the stud's identity. She didn't look abnormal, just a typical unfurnished youngster and of average size for the breed. I booked her in and phoned the manager a few days later. One of the first things I needed to clarify was that, although Rose was the manager who had booked this (not the owner), this little filly would be in her care for at least some time to put into action whatever we came up with. This was confirmed and I went ahead and tuned in with Sophie.

As soon as I had introduced myself to her, I got a searing pulling sensation down the right hand side of my back. I immediately acknowledged this (so the physical feeling would stop) and informed Rose but she said she was not aware of anything physically wrong with the filly. I said that was fine, I would push on and see what else Sophie wanted to say. Instantly she gave me the same pain issue but with that showed me a picture of a mare foaling. I asked Rose if Sophie had been a difficult foaling, but as she had not been born there, she couldn't say either way. This was getting slightly complicated as Rose could not verify facts but I had to continue to repeat what I was being told, in the hope that something would eventually be recognised.

I decided to change tack and asked Sophie to tell me something about herself. I didn't exactly get an 'answer', just a real sense of moroseness and anguish. I pushed further and asked her to tell me what was wrong, or upsetting her, explaining that I could give her a voice to let people know that I was here to help.

She then gave me a vision of a young horse running forward, and then running back, repeating this several times. I described this like a youngster that was really being 'in your face' but being repelled whenever she came forward. At last, this made sense and was confirmed. Sophie's mother had rejected her at four months old and Sophie had felt totally lost and abandoned. She was not in a herd of horses but on her own and was desperately trying to seek attention and affection wherever she could. Unfortunately, comparative to a human being, she was not a little creature but a fairly big animal and had been frightening her owners. Having no motherly figure to love, guide and teach her, her behaviour had become emotionally desperate and erratic. The more she pushed forward for this attention, the more threatening she looked and, therefore the owners did the natural thing, and pushed her away. The older she got, the more indignant she got, and was finding life thoroughly miserable.

So she was now at a large stud, completely overwhelmed and, as much as the staff tried to interact with her, she just didn't want to know. She had no reason to want to trust humans for all she had known was to be pushed away when she had tried to interact. Sophie even pointed out to us that she didn't even mix with the horses in the field, this was again verified. Although she was only two, the staff decided to do a small amount of work with her, in the hope that this would build up some trust, and educate her. She was taught the basics of lunging (getting a horse to move in a circle, attached to a long line, and listen to your voice) but had come to grief when they tried to drive her from behind with the lunge lines. There was a complete entanglement which resulted in hysteria from her and a complete reluctance to let anyone work her from behind again.

The manager asked me to ask her opinion of her being ridden. I was quite amazed when she showed me someone sat on her, and told me that she did not buck or 'have a fit' but walked on gently. This was absolutely how it had happened, so this really did show her geniality, and even more so as I was still aware of her severe discomfort in her back.

By now, we had established why she was being so miserable; she had felt totally rejected by horses and people. She was typically like the child that did not fit in at school and people would have just classed as sulky and expected to 'get on with it'.

She was now talking to me in a more relaxed manner as I had let her get it off her chest, so to speak. I had explained to her that her owners loved her, but were genuinely afraid when this rather large speeding animal came careering up to them, with no apparent idea of its size and strength, and very unsure what she would do. Sophie liked to throw her hind legs up at them and it was not with malicious intent but childish fun, however, unfortunately rather dangerous to anybody in close proximity.

By now, at least we understood why she was acting like she was. So, the next thing for me to do was to try and find out what would make her happier and restore her confidence. In my usual way, I told this manager that I could make no promises she would change but would ask Sophie to see what she thought might help. She said, clear as a bell, to keep telling her she was 'precious' so I repeated the request and was pleasantly surprised when Rose agreed. She also volunteered to pass this onto her staff also! It never ceases to amaze me what requests animals make, but this made perfect sense as this descriptive word was the complete opposite of how she had felt all of her life. I hoped that this word (her bonding key) would help change that. We finished the conversation, complete with the other assurance that, in the future, she would not ever be driven as obviously it would be behind her. Having shown such an abject fear about it, she had been totally unwilling to even try and discuss a solution of how anyone could get round this. I repeated the suggestion that someone have a look at her back as I really felt she had been suffering with it.

I received an email a few weeks later letting me know that she was much happier and the 'precious' word she definitely seemed to be having the desired effect. The chiropractor had indeed found a problem down her right hand side, and bless Sophie, she had stood like a dream to be treated! It was also confirmed that it was not a recent injury but, in fact, rather long term by the changes present. I, myself, believe that this happened during foaling which is why she was keen to show me the pictures of her birth. Most people, myself included, would not have presumed a youngster to have a back problem, but when you think about it, birth can be very strenuous. So it is maybe something to consider if you having issues with a youngster and at least it can be easily eliminated.

HRH

I have had that many conversations with Harry that I don't really know where to start! His owner is Jackie, who most people know as 'Jacks', and to save any confusion with my name for this story she will remain as Jacks. It was Jacks who did some artwork for my last book and has done all the wonderful illustrations in this one. Harry is about sixteen hands, grey and really a law unto himself! But Harry is special, 'special needs' as we sometimes joke, but he is just one of those horses that makes you cry with laughter.

Jacks and her husband Trevor run their tack shop, *The Galloping Gourmet*, in a little place called Marden near Hereford. On the first occasion I had the delight of being 'introduced' to Harry, he spent about an hour expressing how good looking he was and how not so good looking his mates were, and generally making out he was the best horse in the world! Harry is a very clever lad; he looks after Jacks when needed and jumps what is asked of him. But it has to be said, he also takes great joy in just 'putting one in' (bucking) at the right time, and in the right place, and in front of whoever might be watching. Now this watching, mistaken for adoration by him we think, is usually at a local show or the indoor show jumping centre where he thinks he is the 'Kingpin'.

If you don't think horses do things on purpose, believe you me, Harry would be the candidate to convince you otherwise. Get this picture: you are watching the horses warming up at a show and this big grey is clowning about, jumping sideways and looking rather unpredictable to say the least. That is the type of horse that grabs people's interest, especially on a cold winter's day. So, as you head over to the indoor arena encouraging your friends to come and watch this lad 'perform', and blow me, he jumps round sensibly like a true pro! You might wonder how I know all this; do I go and watch him competing? No, he takes utter pleasure in boasting to me, and Jacks, all about it!

On one of the several 'Hello…err Jackie' occasions, Jacks asked me if I could have a word with 'H' as he is often called, as she was having a bit of a problem. She wasn't sure if it was 'him being him' or there actually was a problem. I tuned in with him and, although he was talking like his usual 'chipper' self, he made me aware of being a bit breathless, but not in a serious way. I felt he was just a bit off colour but nothing I could put my finger on so asked him more. He then gave me a picture of him being asked to jump but refusing to go over it, complete with the sound of Jacks moaning at him! Jacks laughed and said at first she thought he was having a bit of a game with her. She then began to think he seemed a bit breathless for a horse that had not really done much exercise. I asked H what was wrong with him and he told me he thought he had a bit of a virus and would need the vet to see him! Jacks thanked me and said she would call the vet straightaway, then go down the field and apologise to him!

She phoned me a few days later and said, "I got the vet and she checked him all over and couldn't find anything obvious so I kept suggesting maybe he had a virus. In the end, she asked me why I thought it was a virus and I told her that he had told you that!" The vet said that *you* were often right and she had come to the same conclusion! He had a few weeks off and was as right as rain. I had a quick catch up with him and he was back to normal, whatever that may be, and asked me to report that Lily, the mare in the next stable, was able to pull his hay-net through to her side and that it was really unfair! His hay-net is now tied on the opposite side, totally out of the reach of Lily.

On the subject of Lily, who is a very pretty bay thoroughbred mare, we thought this hay-net game could actually have been a bit of 'payback', rather than greed. In my last book, I put an 'Animal Titbit' in there about a horse saying, "I'm not sitting in that!" Well, that related to a story from these two. On a lovely summer's day, Jacks had taken H on a fun ride (aptly named as H is a complete show off, safe but a complete show off, nevertheless) and, along with several others, came to a river crossing. They had stopped for a quick rest and to let the horses have a much needed drink when, much to the amazement and hysterics of everyone, H sat down in the water!! Jacks quickly sorted herself out and managed to get him back onto all four feet before he decided to go the whole hog. With all the miles completed and the barbeque eaten, H was then taken home. With great delight, he repeated the whole story to Lily but changed things slightly to suit his own purpose. Now, again, you might wonder how we know this – well, a couple of weeks later when Jacks was riding 'the hay thief',

Lily, she suddenly refused point-blank to enter into the river and this was a river that she had crossed many times before. Another, 'Hello…err Jackie' call to find out why. It took a whole two minutes to discover that H had only gone and told her that the sitting was obligatory! Well, to a horse like Lily this was the unthinkable; even walking through mud at the entrance of a field was beneath her!

A communication was much needed when H decided he did not want to load in the lorry. I bet some of you are thinking, 'This horse sounds like a real toad', but no, you would love him just as much as Jacks and everybody else does. This was their latest lorry and, actually, a lot 'posher' than the old one, but H was having none of it!

I found out that she had driven him to the local show in it and it was only when she went to re-load him that he refused again, and again, but eventually she got him in. She was now at home, it was about four o'clock on a Saturday afternoon (just as well she is a friend!) and having unloaded him she thought it would be a good idea to just quickly try him up the ramp again before turning him out. Bad move in H's eyes, 'No way, José!', he wouldn't budge, so now Jacks didn't know whether to give up or what, but then would he think he had got his own way? I asked him (and please remember I work to the subconscious so you don't generally see any reaction from the horse - you have to hope the message gets through) why did he not want to load? He said he could hear a noise at the back end on the right side of the lorry that sounded unsafe. I asked Jacks if she knew of such a sound and she immediately said that that is where the integrated tack box was and maybe a bucket was banging about.

"No," says H, "I think it is the brakes!"

"I wouldn't have thought so," replied Jacks, "it was checked pre-sale but, to make him happy, I will take it to our local man for the once over!" Meanwhile H is still at the bottom of the ramp, so as a last chance (and to please Jacks) I tried to strike a quick deal, saying, if he went up, stood there for a minute, she would then take him off and he would then go out, but not really expecting it to work, I might add.

Also, he gave the words for her to use, "Right, H, just one minute and you can go out," and incredibly he went up, stood there, turned round and walked calmly back down.

Jacks started to chat and say how amazing was that but I cut her short and said, "I think you better keep up your end of the bargain and take him to the field!"

A few weeks later I got a call from Jacks saying, "I have just had the garage on the phone and H was right about the brakes, the master cylinder had 'gone' and that is why they were making a noise!" I was delighted with this insight from a horse, as was Jacks! So, with brakes fixed and a quick conversation, he now loads without a problem. An amazing result and what was even more astonishing was that this lorry story actually landed up being talked about on Alan Carr's radio show one Saturday night!!

A lady who had been in the tack shop and heard H's lorry tale and was most intrigued so phoned me to ask for help with a mare she had serious problems with. It turned out I knew the exact horse as I had personally met this mare a couple of weeks before! It also turned out to be a day I will not forget in a long time. Rod, a dear friend of ours, is a semi-retired vet and had asked Bob if he could meet him at this farm to do the teeth of the mare in question. Apart from her being rather under nourished, she was absolutely petrified of being handled so would need to be sedated for the procedure. Rod, we know to be excellent with a needle tried to get the injection into her vein but, in spite of being held by the owner's husband and Bob, she somehow managed to swing her front end and lift Rod off his feet and slam him into the whitewashed wall. It was like slow motion with a sickening thud to finish, coupled with a red blood line down the wall. Total panic ensued; we didn't know if she had actually killed him. Incredibly, he just shook himself off, informed us he was alright and got to his feet, albeit a bit shakily. We said enough was enough and the horse would have to wait, but no, Rod being the man he was, insisted that he would dope her as he had never failed before and he wasn't going to start now. Somehow within the next five minutes she was doped and Bob was doing her teeth as fast as he could before she woke up. Rod was now outside on a chair and I had been mopping his head with one of our clean towels and putting some pressure on to stop the bleeding. I had to laugh, once the bleeding had stopped the mare's owner then kept dabbing it with some form of antibacterial that would make most folk wince in a cut, but Rod didn't even seem to notice! With the mare's teeth done, I suggested that I travel in his car to make sure he was okay. Bob would scrub his tools up then follow on to meet and collect me from a pub car park we both knew. Rod and I arrived safely, he was feeling fine so suggested we have a quick drink whilst waiting for Bob, who arrived within ten minutes and had a quick drink too. We laughed, as you do, but heck it was a close call and a day Bob and I won't forget in a hurry, as I am sure neither will Rod!

I did have a chat with the mare that nearly finished off our vet friend, and although we did manage to make a few breakthroughs with her, she also was also refusing to load. In spite of a long communication and every option discussed, our efforts failed. 'Bad to load' horses I find are very tricky to try and change, so I make sure I impress upon people that I cannot promise to make a difference.

In December 2009, when my last book came out, Jacks and Trevor laid on a late evening at the shop and incorporated a book signing, with press in attendance for photographs too. Funnily enough, we had a conversation about looking for missing pets and I explained why I didn't get involved in it. The next day I was travelling up to see a friend of mine and about six o'clock I got a panic phone call from Jacks. "Oh Jackie, can you help me? H and Lily took fright when I was leading them in and have taken off and we cannot find them. We have been searching for an hour and are getting desperate." My mind went into panic but I was suddenly given a picture of grass each side of a drive and a sweeping direction right, and back on itself.

I said, "You know I don't do this but does your neighbour have a long drive with an obvious grass verge?"

"Yes," she exhaled, and I told her not to panic but I think they have doubled back on themselves and gone down their drive instead of yours. I, by this time, was also worrying as I would hate to mislead anyone and you can imagine all scenarios going through my head, let alone Jacks. The funny thing was, I was with my friend Jay who is also psychic/clairvoyant, whatever you want to call us, and she was calmly saying, "It's okay, they are alright!" and went on to repeat it! My guide then kicked in and told me to tell her to calm down and take a bucket of nuts for them to come to. Jacks said a quick thanks and goodbye. At Jay's house I was out of signal so I had an agonising wait until I was travelling back to get news. Phew, I was right; Jacks had left me a message to say they were in the neighbour's garden and were back home safely, none the worse for wear.

You know how you can 'laugh after the fact'? Well, Jacks told me the whole story. Apparently, in the pitch dark she went to her neighbour's rather grand house, stood in the porch, knocked on the door and said, "Sorry to bother you, but you don't happen to have seen my two horses, have you?"

"No, sorry," he replied, "I haven't seen or heard a thing!" With that, Jacks happened to rattle the bucket and these two horses just appeared, up his lawn, *under* the washing line and made a beeline for the bucket. As they jostled to push each other's heads out of the bucket, Jacks just stood there not knowing whether to laugh or cry, and apologised profusely for the mess she knew their hooves would have made of his lawn. The horses happily went back down their own drive and settled themselves down for the night - as if nothing out of the ordinary had happened!

Back to Basics

Fiona is one of my clients who is also very holistic herself. When the email came through, I presumed it would be to talk to another of her horses, but, no, it was actually for her cat, Verity. This cat (so beautifully named I had to remark on it) was a tortoiseshell with a big white 'bib' on the front of her. Fiona thought she would be about eleven or twelve years old; this being an educated guess as she had had her eight years and the re-homing centre reckoned she was about three years old when she came to them. Her email expressed concern, saying that Verity was acting oddly so I booked her in as quickly as I could.

I tuned in with Verity and she told me that she was not a needy cat and, 'Just got on with life!' And sure enough, she was an independent girl but at this point was really feeling out of sorts. She immediately showed me a spurt of dark liquid vomit and Fiona replied saying that she had been vomiting but didn't recognise the dark colour bit. Suddenly then it clicked, she had cleaned up 'something', but was not sure what it had been, but we both knew! Verity then made me feel very anxious, and gave me a vision of going back and forth to her cat litter tray; again, Fiona confirmed this, and I said she made me think she had cystitis or something along those lines. Since I had started talking to Verity I was aware of an uncomfortable pressure on the left side of my head, sort of behind my eye. I warily asked if she was squinting her left eye, but Fiona said she had not noticed. I said not to worry but, as she was going to the vet, he could maybe check her eyes as well. Fiona asked me to ask Verity why had she started crying, and especially at night - the way a female cat would wail. Fiona had even been getting up to attend to her as she was sounding very distressed. I asked her cat and she said that she wasn't sad but just 'didn't feel right', so we left it at that.

As I have said many times, I do get to feel physical problems, and sometimes, as on this occasion, I was given a taste as well. This tasted weird, and horrid really, rather metallic coupled with an acrid smell. I asked if her breath smelled and Fiona confirmed it did, and as I was trying to explain what I was tasting, Verity gave the words 'ketosis'. I immediately repeated it, and said, "I vaguely remember this term and think it is to do with liver/kidney function? But if you hang on a second, I will look it up on the computer." I Googled it, and sure enough it was that, so I suggested that maybe she should ask the vet for a blood test. Fiona said that Verity was not very keen on being handled by the vets, and as we were on the subject, could I ask her about her carcinoma (cancer) lump removal and what she has to say about it? First of all, she went to the wrong leg and showed a fighting scar instead, but when she got to the right place, Verity seemed totally unconcerned about it and said, "It has popped out like a pea!"

So now we had a good outline of what was going on, I asked her if she had any idea of the cause, and Verity basically informed us that she did in fact prefer the ordinary dry biscuits and would be better on them. "Oh", said Fiona, "I had changed her on to the sachets of soft food and have given her less biscuits, as she was getting older, so I thought they would be better for her." Then the penny dropped, it was not long after this that the crying started, but to be honest, food would be the last thing that most owners would associate with a cat starting to cry. Fiona asked if she should say to the vets that she had been talking to me, and I suggested probably not as some vets really don't 'get' what I do. I suggested she put it across like she'd thought of it herself and ask if any blood tests would be possible.

Within the week, Fiona came back to me and this is how her email went:

'Hi Jackie, here's an update on Verity:

I changed her diet back to the old one and this has made an immediate difference with her symptoms, she's peeing and crying a lot less and seems happier in herself. She seems to have stopped the really distressing crying, the night-time yowling, altogether.

She's had urine and blood tests done; the urine did show cystitis and the blood work showed liver (that may be the ketosis) and kidney damage, she'll now start on medication and a prescription diet to help with maintaining her kidney function. The vet couldn't find anything in her left eye. I'm suspecting that the pressure in her head was linked to her bladder/kidney dysfunction. However, once she's been on her new tablets and diet I was wondering whether you could do a brief 'check-in' with her to ask specifically about how she's feeling in her head. Can you let me know if you'd be happy to do that please?

Many, many thanks again, your work is SO valuable at finding out how the animal is feeling and I'm very grateful for what you do. It is such a great way to fast-track getting the right sort of help when you literally hear it from the horse's (cat's) mouth!

Warm wishes,
Fiona'

I had the quick 'check-in' with Verity a couple of weeks later and she was really upbeat and back to her normal self, and apparently the stinging had stopped when she was peeing. Fiona said she had started playing again and seemed so much brighter and happier. I let her pass me any physical feelings and had to be honest and say I still could feel slight pressure on the left hand side of my head, but much less than before. I said, to be honest, she is senior in years and if there was something going on, it might have been happening for a long time, but at present it is not causing her distress. When she was ill with her other problems, it did feel worse, but you know yourself if you are feeling poorly, everything seems heightened in its sensations. I did ask Fiona what the vets had said when she had somehow got them to check Verity's eye and, they said basically the same as me - if there was something, it is showing no symptoms now, and if problems do develop then they can discuss the various options then.

I was so pleased she was back to normal and, obviously, Fiona was delighted too, and long may it stay that way.

Handle with Care

Never has a horse been so well named as Apollo, who was a Belgium Warmblood; big and handsome, a flashy chestnut with just that 'something' about him. This ten-year-old dressage horse oozed class, but his new owner, Susie, a fairly experienced horse-woman, was having horrendous problems with him.

I had done work for a friend of hers so she contacted me hoping that I could find out what was going on, and hopefully do something about it. Susie decided to go up to the stables where he was kept and chat to me on her mobile from there. I tuned in with him and really didn't expect the reaction I got. Angry, he was totally irate and spoke to me in a very staccato fashion, as if the ends of his words had been chopped off, or by finishing his sentences with a sarcastic, "Don't they?!"

He was kicking the door and lunging forward at Susie, who interrupted me saying, "He has just tried to have another 'go' at me."

I suggested she step back and I tried to talk to him again, but I was just getting a burble of, "Get out of my way, I don't want to know, go away, just go away!" I asked logically if she had rescued this horse (as that would take us in an obvious direction) but, no, she had bought him, and paid well for him at that!

I asked Susie if she had bought the horse knowing he was like this and she explained, "He was good as gold when I tried him, and sweet as anything!" The thoughts running through my head were: 'Was he doped and now back to his wide awake self?' But even if doped they do not become 'sweet' when it wears off if they are not that way inclined. I said I would ask him more and see what I could find out.

He burst in with, "She promised she wouldn't sell me, in fact she swore she wouldn't, but she did and, for less than she wanted!" I repeated these fairly venomously 'spat' words at me and this was actually spot on. His previous owner, his breeder, had no intention of ever selling him but had decided to emigrate and as much as she wanted to keep him, it just wasn't practical. She had sold all the other horses but had intended not to part with him as she adored him and had competed well with him. She had, in fairness, found a loan home for him and he was very well behaved but the lady didn't have time for him and her two children, so returned him after a few months. I understood why he might feel aggrieved as the loan home had returned him but explained that he now had a lovely new permanent home with Susie. I told him how delighted she had been buy him and that she had indeed, bought him cheaper at five thousand when his owner had really wanted nearer seven! He was not worth less; this was only because his owner just wanted him to go to a good home and was running out of time before she emigrated. This information was irrelevant to him as he was fuming and as far as he was concerned, "That was it, I can't trust anybody, I am not going to let her close because then I can't be hurt or disappointed, full stop!" complete with rearing pictures and plenty of teeth gnashing for me to see. Well, that told us and as much as I tried to reason with him but felt like I was talking to a brick wall. He eventually said he understood (I think to get rid of me) so at that point I thought I would ask other things. He, needless to say, didn't want to do small talk, but did tell me about his great paces although he felt rather sore in his rump muscles. This could have also been an explanation as to why he had 'exploded' whilst being ridden and promptly thrown Susie off, although, judging by his temper, I would not have liked to hazard a guess as to where the truth behind that lay. Susie said she would take on board about the rump area but when she informed me that he actually had bitten her, and not just a little nip. I suggested she be extremely careful with him as he was a very big and very angry horse. I said my goodbyes and wished her the best but thought it was a rather worrying situation to say the least.

Two days later, and I get an email, complete with payment, saying Apollo was still trying to bite her and 'having a go' but she would like me to try again. Now if I am honest, my heart sank because as much as I had stated that I cannot 'make' any animal change that didn't want to, I really thought this was probably an example of that. But I give Susie her due, she really did not want to just give up on him as what was she to do? Although she had paid a lot of money for him and he was at present pretty non-sellable, she knew that underneath there was a nice horse that she had previously met, so at the moment she was in a no win situation anyway.

I tuned in again and although he was still doing his 'mechanical question ending' but to a slight lesser degree. He still wanted nothing to do with people (us humans that had cheated him) but suggested he be turned away with some youngsters out in the field, and to be left alone to 'stew in his own juice', as he put it. I checked if that would be possible and Susie said she thought it would. By the use of his 'stewing' remark we noted that, at least he was registering that he was angry so that was a tiny step forward. I again explained to him that he was in fact punishing the one person that wants to love him and is totally innocent of everything that he perceived to be a human let down. Susie said she would contact me in a few months when she started to try and handle him again. In the field she was going to make a conscious effort just to feed him, give him hay and as little else possible. This way hopefully he would not feel under any pressure and maybe it would dawn on him that she was maybe a good person after all.

Two months passed and Susie sent me a text to ask to arrange an update with him, and could she call me from her mobile as she was going out at lunchtime but that day and time suited her. It was actually a Sunday, but I made an exception for her knowing the history. I tuned in to him, and amazingly he was quite chatty and seemed a lot happier in himself. "He is," Susie said, "he really has changed and although he is still rather dominant and stallion-like he was in fact much like the horse I'd originally bought!"

I asked him if he had enjoyed his break and what had it done for him? He had been turned out with a bunch of riding school horses that apparently were quick to inform him that some of them had already had several homes and he was lucky he was only on his second! That really had an impact on him and his temper diminished quite rapidly. He also told me that he had treatment for his pelvis as Susie thought he looked worse behind, and, he was so well behaved whilst being physically manipulated. Susie said she had warned the physio how bad he could be, which any responsible person would (but believe you me, some people don't!) but he had stood there and let her treat him with no resistance at all. He did admit though, that he did try to nip her, as he still does to Susie, but not in a 'bad way'. I was quite staggered and said how pleased and amazed I was. At this point she still had not ridden him but could I possibly pass an apology on to him. I did say she could do it herself, as he understands what she says but then she explained what had happened.

Susie's family, and the yard owner, had put pressure on her to sell this horse during the first few months at his angry stage, as they feared for her safety. He was advertised and at a very reasonable price for such a well bred horse that has done superb dressage. Susie had been working away and somebody had responded to her advert some two months later. Susie explained to this prospective buyer that she had turned him away and was waiting to see if he would 'chill out' but this woman was insistent that she come and look at him anyway. She persuaded Susie that this would be a sensible idea should Susie decide to sell him after all should he not have changed after his field rest.

As I said, Susie was away from home and eventually got bamboozled into agreeing to let this woman go to the yard to see him. It was made clear she could see him move, but on no uncertain terms was she to try and ride him. So Susie arranged for one of the livery yard staff to catch him, take him into the school so this woman could see how he moved; just loose, not ridden. Undeterred this woman travelled a long way and arrived at the yard with saddle and bridle! She asked to see him and then proceeded to tack him up, much to the curiosity of the yard owner. They presumed that there must have been a change of plan and that Susie had agreed for her to try riding him. After all you wouldn't just take it upon yourself to do so would you? Well, actually yes, this woman did precisely that! So regardless of having no permission from Susie, she took him in the school and rode him round! I stopped Susie there and said I would ask Apollo what he thought, before she went any further, and his reply astounded me, "Well, I didn't buck her off did I?"

I hoped this was the case and Susie said, "True, he didn't." Apollo then went on to slate the woman's riding, who was a complete 'know-all', was very rough and ready and with a sarcastic imitation of her saying, 'This is how you treat them. I've been in horses all my life!'

My brain immediately sprung into action and pointed out to Susie not to feel guilty, this was not of her own making, but actually this woman was Apollo's test dummy! Susie laughed and said it was a good way of thinking about it. So, if this woman had ridden him so shoddily and he was gracious enough not to dump her, then why should he want to throw Susie off when she rode him with thought and care? Apollo informed us that Susie had nothing to apologise for and then swallowed his pride and apologised for his angry behaviour.

He also took the opportunity to inform us he had now decided to forgive his previous owner too!

Wow, what a turn-around and Susie said she would be in touch after she had ridden him for a while. The bizarre thing was this whole conversation took place while she was sitting in a pub on that Sunday lunchtime. She had discreetly sat in the corner scribbling her notes, and I just giggle to think, I bet no one knew she was actually chatting with her horse!

Panic - within a month Susie was distraught as Apollo had gone very lame on the off hind leg, and the vets had said that they thought he had a serious hock problem and he would probably never come sound. Apollo totally disagreed, so I quickly said my usual, 'remember I don't diagnose, I can only tell you what they say' and he is saying that is it higher up, in the sacroiliac region, and that it *will* mend. Susie said she would get a physio out to him and would come back to me in a couple of weeks to let me know if he had been right or wrong. Guess what... he was right and was now about ninety percent sound, and…Susie had started riding him ever so gently. He was being good, not a hundred percent good, he still was being quirky; he was being obstinate for the sake of it really enjoying trying to assert his dominance, but on the whole was being a good boy really.

As time has passed, Apollo has become a wonderful riding horse, definitely not a novice ride but he has started jumping and enjoying that as well. Susie has kept in touch and even sent me a beautiful photograph of them together with her arm wrapped up around his neck. They both looked so relaxed and happy- not bad for a horse that had been attacking her previously! For fun we also at one point decided to ask him, "If you had a choice, what name would you have chosen?"

And his answer: "Il Domini!" ('He dominates' in English) well, that says it all doesn't it! But this horse in careful hands is fine; he cannot be bullied but to be encouraged to see where the boundaries of acceptance are. Susie has no intentions of parting with him and I give her such credit for one so young for seeing through all the anger and being determined to try and get through to the real horse underneath. I also thank her for trusting me with such a difficult case, and I do think, to be honest, we were very fortunate that he did revert back to his own true self, because often when a horse has got to the stage of striking out and biting at whoever comes near, sadly, sometimes things can't be undone. So then the cycle continues, as they get passed on from person to person, branded, vicious, dangerous etc. (Don't get me wrong, some are, just as people can be, this is just a fact of life. But often, as with people, something has happened and set off a chain reaction in their life causing them to become callous and mean, but sometimes it is just their personality. I try my best to look on people like that with pity, as that is as far away from my understanding of self-happiness as it gets). With Susie as his owner, and having 'perseverance' for a middle name I hope their relationship continues to blossom and she gets to compete him as she had originally bought him to do.

"Please tell Emily she is my world and I am glad to be a part of hers."
Words spoken straight from a pony's heart.

"Turning the TV up doesn't make the football any better!"
An English Bull Terrier's message for his owner's husband.

"I am a total enigma, just when you thought you had taught me something, I go and do the complete opposite.
A very honest description of a horse that really doesn't do 'consistent!'

"It's okay, it's only horse handstands!"
A horse's answer when trying to ask him to be more careful when bucking and plunging in his field.

Jackie Weaver

Acclimatising

I do like it when I chat to people with a distinct accent or dialect. One of my clients, Jess, is from Delaware, USA, and is a wonderful and extremely patient animal lover; she also makes me hoot with her 'Americanisms' and funny notes on the end of emails.

Jess contacted me as she, and her husband, had rescued their first Greyhound, a four-and-a-half year old ex-race, that she had christened Rainy. Jess is a member of an internet forum, aptly named, *Greyt Expectation Greyhound Rescue*, who do fantastic work and, as their website says, 'Finding the Right Homes for Retired Hounds in the Delaware, Maryland, D.C. Virginia area…and Beyond!!' This takes huge dedication and obviously works, as their site is full of charming pictures of the Greyhounds with their new owners. Jess had seen some stuff written about me on there and as she was experiencing problems with her new pet, so emailed me for help. Ex-racing Greyhounds, I know from experience, do make wonderful pets, but often they have no idea of what home-life entails and require a great deal of empathy and understanding to help them adjust.

Some clients are kind enough to write out their notes for me, and Jess had written the reading out that I did for Rainy, in its entirety for others *GEGR* forum to digest! I honestly don't mind when people do this as it actually validates my work, although there can be some very narrow minded rude people who take great joy in mocking what we do. So Jess just emailed me the complete compilation of all her forum write-ups along with her comments and thoughts at the time. I have decided to write this in the same way that she gave her notes back to me, narrated by Jess herself with some translation and comments by me, which for ease of reading, I will put in italics, until I let you know it is me talking again.

Jess writes: We started off the conversation and Rainy sent Jackie a picture of a deck and her looking through the wooden slats. I don't have a deck, so that might have been at a previous stop for her? Then Jackie saw a wicker basket full of dogs' toys. I don't have a wicker basket for Rainy's toys; I have a plastic dollar store laundry hamper, so another swing and a miss there! By this point I was thinking, 'what a kook'...*(nearest translation in English would be nutty!)* but when I let Rainy's foster Mom know, she said that she keeps her dog toys in a wicker basket and has a red deck! What are the odds?

Rainy told us she liked our calm house but everything was a big step for her and that she was unsure of where she is allowed to go in the house. This made sense – when we are there, she usually only stays on her dog bed in the living room, or the other dog bed in our bedroom. I told Jackie that Rainy is allowed anywhere in the house including on our bed and the sofa if she wanted. Rainy's response was, "Are you for real?" The very next day after this conversation Rainy started wandering around more, sniffing, even sticking her head in when we opened the fridge!

Rainy was also confused about getting hand-fed treats that were offered to her. Jackie then asked me if she was a working dog before we got her, (*I did not realise at that point she had raced*) but Jackie said those working dogs probably aren't familiar with treats. Rainy also said that sometimes she's not sure if she's allowed to eat her own supper! She does hesitate sometimes and I have to tell her to eat and stop being goofy. Jackie assured Rainy that if we give her something it is for HER.

Unfortunately, one of Rainy's problems was that she was clawing at the doors as if to escape so, sensibly, Jess kept her in a dog cage while they were out of the house. Rainy then said that she thinks she drinks too much! She does tend to drink for long times instead of going back a few times to grab a sip. Jackie told me that Rainy is worried about the bowl being empty and us not filling it. Rainy no longer gets water in her crate because she chewed and destroyed the snap on the water container that we got for her and, as she digs up her bed, she tips water bowls over. She usually runs straight to her water bowls and guzzles like a camel every time she's let out of her crate. I always assumed she was thirsty from stress panting, although she seemed fine in herself, and is not in the crate for more than 4 hours at a time. Here's the creepy (*thanks, Jess!!*) part. That same afternoon she stopped guzzling when let out of the crate and, hasn't done it since! A behaviour that has been happening for a month and a half then suddenly stops? Coincidence?

Rainy also said she was scared to try to do things for fear of getting yelled at, which did match her personality! Rainy requested that when she does something wrong to tell her, "No, please don't," instead of raising our voices. HOLY BATMAN, it works! If she is sniffing at our dinner plates, a quiet, "No, please don't," makes her go lay on her dog bed. One day Rainy was licking the outside of a ketchup bottle in the fridge door, and a, "No, please don't," made her walk away! The weird part is that you don't even have to put a negative inflection in your tone, you can singsong it and she will listen.

Jackie asked her, "Do you hurt anywhere?" We got a mention about her right front foot. Rainy said she's very careful that no one steps on her right foot and that her shoulder had hurt at one time, but nothing hurts right now. Rainy then told Jackie she was especially careful about her right front while on walks. Chris (*Jess's husband*) said that he noticed when she sniffs around, she keeps her weight on her left front and her right front shakes a little. I always just figured it was excitement about being out and sniffing new smells.

"What do you think of the cats?" I got Jackie to ask. Rainy is amazed at how rough they play and that her job was to avoid the cats. How many times have I uttered this exact phrase - at least 50 times! This came out before I told Jackie that Rainy tried to eat Frizzle (*one of her two cats*).

I got Jackie to ask, "Why do you cry during the day?" She said she was crying during the day because she's lonely, but is very happy that she gets to sleep with us and is not crated at night like she used to be. She says she's a lot less lonely than she was at the track. Rainy said she likes the music that we play for her all day and she even sometimes can hear it in her sleep! Rainy said she's okay in her crate and not to worry about her. Jackie also asked Rainy how she would describe herself.

Rainy said, "Gentle, and I would be very loyal if I knew how to be." How cute is that?!

Overall it was about an hour conversation. I am convinced it is real. All the immediate sudden changes are amazing. They can't all be coincidences. She has cut her whining time during the day in half, and has stopped the major stress panting. When I put her in the crate in the morning she lays right down instead of standing there panting until I leave. She is in general more cheerful, adventurous, and relaxed.

This is back to me, Jackie, talking again – Apart from Jess being an absolute pleasure to chat to, and hear her thoughts afterwards, I was delighted with the change in Rainy. She is now a relaxed housedog, and, uncharacteristically (due to their chase-the-furry-item training) is being as good as gold about the cats too. With Jess and her husband having fallen in love with this Greyhound, Rainy, next to appear – Sunshine, a two-year-old this time, that they had only had for a week. She was a Fawn Greyhound, but not a Red Fawn like Rainy, and the other difference was that Sunshine was more 'off the track' than Rainy had been. So, having spent very little time at the foster home, she knew even less about everyday life than Rainy had. As you will read, in Jess's words, Sunshine was far more complicated and a challenge for them, and for me!

Now back to Jess's write up: Sunshine started out by saying that she was very agitated and confused, and wanted to know if nuzzling our hand was good? (She would run up and sniff our hands real quick, then run off). (*I explained that this was fine and an affectionate sign that would be reciprocated*) - Sunshine has now started coming up to us more often. She sadly informed us that if someone didn't have her then she would be put down - this we assume is what she thought before *GEGR* snatched her up. Sunshine gave Jackie the feeling of a stress headache and then wanted to know when she's moving on from this place - oh, how sad. She doesn't understand why she's here and kept asking over and over, "Why was I moved?" - this being about her short adoption stay then on to us. Then she offered up that there is nothing physically wrong with her! (We knew that from the vet trip on Friday!) She requested 'sweet flower drops' in her water, which we thought meant Rescue Remedy.

One major obstacle to overcome was her toilet training, referred to as 'potty training', or 'to potty' when they do 'go', in Jess's American lingo.

When asked about being clean in the house, Jackie said that Sunshine seems to have no concept of the potty training and explained to her that she is only allowed to potty when she can see the sky.(*I have used this before, and it has worked, but have check first if they have skylights or a see-through roof!)* Then if she potties anywhere else, it's like pottying in a bedroom instead of going the bathroom to do it, which would be very wrong. Sunshine also gave words for us to tell her to remind her. Jackie also asked Sunshine if she wanted to stay with us and she replied with, "I would love to stay if they want me." I said of course we wanted her and, like a little kid, Sunshine asked, "Why?" So I said that she was super-cute, so sweet, and the kitties liked her, and that Rainy needed a sister, and we want her in our family. She wants to be told that she is here to stay and that she is special. Also she wants some St John's Wort in with her dinner to help her headache. I explained that she's on meds from the vet so we can't give her that. Jackie asked if the meds from the vet were changing anything or working. And Sunshine replied, "Not one bit! No effect at all!" (I kinda agree, so will have to see about that one). I asked if Sunshine wanted to go out to the park and do stuff like that? "If I'm going out with you and coming back with you, then I can brave it!" Sunshine wanted to make sure the lady from the rescue didn't say she was a nightmare. She said that she felt safe and not afraid of the lady, so would prove she can be a good girl, she just needs time. *(This was confirmed, so I thought a very sensible and positive comment).* At the end of the talk, Sunshine said she understands a lot more now!

Things with Sunshine have improved slowly since chatting with her. I'm going to try and schedule another chat with both pups sometime in a few months! We finished the call.

This is me, Jackie, talking again. As we know, every dog is different and that also applies to how receptive they are to a communication. A very high percentage change, but there are some that don't. Sunshine has improved, but is still showing nervous behaviour, but I hope with time that she will settle like Rainy, who found it so easy to do. I did have the later reading with them both, and even read their 'blog' of their summer vacation that Jess had emailed me a link to. They looked like two very happy and relaxed children!

A year later, Rainy was lame and they needed to restrict her exercise. I had a chat with her, and got the indication of an old crack in her toe on her right foot (the foot she was protective of, that she made us aware of previously!) I explained things to her, and she thought she would be okay in three weeks. An email popped through a few weeks later – panic! I will let Jess take over from here:

Hey Jackie, Rainy's sprained toe is doing much better. She's been sound on it for two weeks now and I'm going to wait another week, or two, before we start going for decent walks again. No running at the dog park for a bit since she doesn't know how to take it easy! But, help! Sunshine has had a big backslide in her phobia of the world. The vet started her on Prozac two days ago since she has been refusing to go out for potty walks. She's still her crazy puppy self inside the house, but as soon as we get leashes, harnesses, collars, or dog coats out she shuts down and just lies there shaking. Then we have to physically drag her 56lb hiney (*American slang for bum*) down the hallway and outside. Phew, what a workout! Hopefully the medicine will kick in soon. The vet said it could take up to four weeks! It's so hard to see her not feeling comfortable in her own skin outside. I think our massive amount of snow might be getting her more nervous since she can't see over the huge snow piles to make sure there are no puppy-eating humans there! Plus she's getting less exercise which probably isn't helping her anxiety - a tired pup is usually a happy one! As soon as I can get some more dollars we need to schedule another appointment with Sunshine. I finally read your book (*Animal Insight*) and it is AWESOME! I couldn't put it down and read it all in one day. I laughed and cried and had such a happy fuzzy feeling from reading it!

Back to me, Jackie, for a moment. I decided to have a quick word with Sunshine and email it over to Jess, as she sounded desperate. Sunshine told me that she was so confused as everything had changed and she was very nervous for reasons like - where would the cars drive? They would not know where the roads were, and more importantly, where the pavements were that she would be walking on. She also expressed to me how unnervingly bright it was, which got me to ask if maybe in their house it is quite dark by comparison? I told her that it will all go back to normal some time, and that Jess would never let any harm come to her.

So, back to Jess's email: Thanks so much for the info on Sunshine! We do keep our house pretty dark and it is very bright with the sun reflecting off the snow. I'll try opening the curtains more to let more light inside so it's not as much of a shock to her. It makes sense that she would be scared to walk outside since there are no sidewalks anymore with all this snow, and doesn't look like it's going to melt anytime soon either! I thought we were over all this extreme fear stuff; just as well she is so cute!! Thanks, and I'll let you know how Sunshine is doing in a few weeks. I can't thank you enough! (*We laughed at the fact that although they were both named after a type of weather, that a different type again could cause such a problem!*)

The very next day, she sent another email: You're a miracle worker!!! Last night, and this morning, she was still hesitant but no dragging needed! If she does get a bit stuck on our walk, I just singsong

"Nothing to fear," and she marches along with us! We even went for a walk in the park last night and she was perfect! Thank you. Thank you. *But the next day, another email:* We've just realised - she won't potty in the snow! *I had a quick word, and, yes, we got that one sorted too!*

As you can gather, Sunshine is no easy task as she is naturally nervous and suspicious, but she does listen to me, (thank goodness!) this is confirmed by the sign off - We really need weekly therapy sessions with you! Hopefully things will keep going in the right direction. I can't thank you enough!

Thanks, Jess.

I have since also had the pleasure of talking to one of her cats, Murdoch. Murdoch was nine years old, tabby and white, and had been exhibiting a long term 'problem'. He would eat and then throw up, but not just on the odd occasion like many cats; this was a very regular occurrence. Jess took him to the vet but there didn't seem to be anything physically wrong with him. He assured me he was not thin, which was true so I asked him if he knew why it happened. "Oh, it's just because I'm greedy and scoff my food so fast it comes right back up!" And with a slight tone of sincerity he added, "There is a name for it you know," he drawled.

"Is there?" I keenly enquired, "Yes, it's called, Murdoch syndrome!" Well, we cracked up laughing guessing he was really trying to let us know – 'ask a silly question and you will get a silly answer!' Having now got to know Jess and her animals, having a cat with a wicked sense of humour would be nothing out of the norm! Actually, come that – there is not much in my life seems out of the norm, well, to me anyway!!

Chinese Whispers

As you have gathered, I get to talk to animals all over the world and not just thanks to my use of telepathy but the fabulous technological breakthroughs like the internet and video calling features too. One such foreign call that springs to mind was a cat in China.

It was winter time in 2007 and I had completely lost my voice, whilst this was a true blessing for my husband, I really couldn't work! I had postponed everybody for a couple of weeks but then a reading came in that I just felt needed to be done. My instinct was right; this cat had been exported to China about two weeks previously and was anxious in her new environment. I had, by this time, rested my voice for a few days and managed to master the 'loud' whisper, so actually did the whole communication in this whispering fashion. As the little ditty on my website says about this: It gave a whole new meaning to Chinese whispers!

But seriously, this cat, Smudge, had been distressed having been flown out to China and was showing real signs of anxiety, so Bev was hoping that I could talk to Smudge to help her settle in better. She emailed her picture and details, and the photo was of a gorgeous little black cat with beautiful amber eyes. She was nearly two and a half and although the China move was never meant to be a permanent one, they were going to be there long enough that they wanted her to be with them.

I tuned into her and she made me feel so anxious and gave me that repetitive feeling you would see with an angst caged animal. In my best loud whisper I tried to explain what I was looking at and how she made me feel. It turned out, bizarrely she was licking the blinds (and curtains) in a rhythmical action and so much so that when they tried to distract her she would go back and continue to do so. She was very fearful as they were now in a flat, as opposed to their house in Scotland where she had been used to going in and out. Bev explained that unfortunately that would definitely not be possible here. At this point in time, she would not have wanted to anyway, as she was frightened by the sounds of other strange cats around, which Bev confirmed that she had seen, and heard too. I told Smudge that she had nothing to fear from the other cats and they could not come into her flat, "...so please rest assured that you are safe." Previously she had been quite happy to 'meet and greet' visitors, but she was now treating new people all with suspicion. This was all tied in with her stressful anxieties - she was just totally bewildered. I asked her what would make her life better and she said that she wanted ping pong balls to play with again. Bev said that Smudge had played with some back home and she would go and get some for her.

Smudge really wanted to know how long they would be there, and why?! The first we could not really answer but told her it was a contract that they had and when finished, the intention was to return to Britain and buy a house. With that she perked up and said, "I would like one with a conservatory!!"

I asked if their previous house had a conservatory on it, and the answer was, "No." Bev said that Smudge was a real 'window sunbather', so maybe that is why. Smudge was told if they could get a house with a conservatory, they would, just for her! I wished them well, well 'whispered' them well and hoped she would settle down.

I didn't hear anything for a long time but Bev came back to me a year later for another reading. She made me laugh by saying, "Nice to hear you this time!"

I told her that Smudge said, "People are less scary now!" I didn't really know her personality as previously she was so stressed it had not been evident. She was not the chattiest of cats and, to be honest, I think the owner might have been a bit disappointed. I can only say it like they do, however little or however much, I can't change things as that would be dishonest and not what the animal is like, or being like to me anyway Smudge was one of these cats that one day is all over you, and then another day she doesn't want to know. She stressed to me several times that she was happy, although was still licking the curtains (but not the blinds) but in a way like using a comfort blanket, and didn't really want to stop! Smudge thought they had been in China for longer than they had planned and this was actually correct. She was assured that they would be returning to Europe, but not sure when or where to. We discussed the business of her flying, and she simply said she wanted to be told that they would be there to meet her. Now she at least knew why she was travelling and that they would be re-united, and maybe one day she might even get her own conservatory!

Return of the Viking

When it comes to dentistry my husband has the 'patience of Job', but some push the boundaries and Thor was one of them. Don't get me wrong, he is not mean or violent, but a strong black Fell pony with a will to match his build. We first met Thor many years ago when he lived in an area of Wales quite near to us, and he was a bit of a lad, to say the least. I had written his name as 'Thaw' on his dental form which I thought was a rather strange choice, but Bob smiled and then gave me a quick history lesson. Apparently Thor, according to Norsk mythology, was the 'God of thunder'! We wondered how apt the name would be, and once we had met him, I reckoned Thor knew more about history than me and was trying to live up to his name! The routine work doing horse's teeth requires the filing off sharp edges and most horses stand there as good as gold as it is usually a painless procedure. But then you get to meet the others like Thor, who just decide they don't want it done, whatever! I was still holding the horses for Bob then, and he really did give us a run for our money, so we were quite relieved when the owners, with their beloved Thor, moved away. Like a bad penny, five years later he turned back up in Bob's working area. He was now with a family, who, like the previous owners, loved him to bits, but found his thoughts on dentistry had not altered one iota! As I have said, he is not violent; he is just damn awkward and gathers momentum as he tries to push his way out of the situation, giving us the perfect example of 'thundering around'. Nowadays, to make life easier for him and everyone, the vet sedates him so Bob can work on him safely.

Thor is now in his mid-twenties and I always enquire after him when Lucy, his owner, books him in. He is such a monkey but the type you can't help but laugh at. So, when she booked him for me to talk to, I laughed and said, "I can't believe this, first we thought we had got away with doing his teeth and now I am going to talk to him! Actually I will say, I do think we will be in for some fun," and I was right! She said that she wanted this done as soon as possible as she was getting desperate, and would send the photo through as soon as possible.

On my standard email I try to cover all that people need to know, and it used to say, 'send a photo of your animal, (it can be old).' However, I did receive a few with pictures of animals in the far distance that were fairly indistinguishable! So I then changed the wording slightly to encourage people to do a closer version to: 'preferably so I can see their eyes', and guess what? I kid you not; someone sent me a picture of their horse's eye!! So now it reads, 'but preferably with its face to me' and that is exactly what Lucy sent me, but, in her rush sent me one with Thor wearing a full length face mask! I was one that resembled the cloth ones that horses used to wear going into battle, so I couldn't see who he was anyway! I found this hilarious, and sent her back a note asking if I could have one in which I could see his face? I also commented that if Thor had got to choose one himself, the one I have received would probably have been his witty choice anyway.

I introduced myself (well, re-introduced myself to be precise) and he was quick to introduce himself back. "Hello, I am a big boy, you know," came his reply, which threw me slightly as I never thought of him as that big. I knew he was a pony not a horse, but nevertheless I remarked that was interesting to know and what else did he want to say. "It is not my fault, I don't know where my feet are!" came his reply, which I repeated to Lucy.

She burst out laughing and said, "That's him, he is so clumsy, he has actually tripped and fallen into his stable before now!" I laughed too at the thought of him stumbling in his stable, shaking himself off and carrying on as if nothing had happened. I said to Lucy that he is under the impression that he is a 'big boy' but I know he is only a pony but he draws himself as much bigger too.

"Oh but he *is*, well, for a Fell," she replied. "He is 14.2 hands and that is way over the height for a Fell pony.

He smiled upon hearing this and then gave me the funniest picture of him sitting like a dog! "Spot on!" she declared. "He does, but is it because he struggles to get up, or is he in pain?"

"I don't get that impression, but I shall ask him." I was right; it was for complete effect and showing off, as he would, so he gave me a little video replay of his comedy routine He would roll, then push himself up onto his bottom with front legs fully stretched out in front of him, and sit there long enough to be noticed, and then nonchalantly get up, having said to himself, "Okay, I think that is long enough!" What a complete attention seeker and poser he was!

Next was him curling his top lip, and Lucy exclaimed, "He is always doing it, he is such a laugh!"

He kept making me feel itchy and then showed me him rubbing his neck up and down on the stable's door-frame; Lucy acknowledged this and said could I ask him more about it. He presented me with a picture of a horse seriously rubbing on a tree, then on a fence post, and so hard that I actually said I thought the fence might break. "It has," she said, "once he did it with such force, it collapsed and this is why I have come to you." Thor had developed severe itching and was rubbing his heels and scratching his body so badly that I could see the lesions and pus pustules on him.

He started to make me feel quite anxious and unsettled, which equated to him never really being able to relax, due to the constant annoyance of the flies. He said, "I am only comfortable when it rains," which was a strange thing to say and Lucy said she thought he was worse when it rained as the flies come out even more. But, if you take it literally what he had said, when it is actually raining, there are no flies flying around him but, sadly though, they do then come back with a vengeance. I realised now how distressing this situation was getting for him and Lucy and her family, as he was not just loved by her, but also her husband and her mum. He was really the family pony and was so genuine to ride and generally kept everybody amused. They had tried simply everything on the market to help him and when I asked what he thought would help, he replied, "I think the cattle stuff will work!" I didn't expect that answer and passed it over to Lucy to see if it made any sense to her, and it did. Her vet was using a drug that has shown success on horses to treat bovine[1] flies, and had actually had the first in his course of injections and was maybe slightly better, but it was too soon to show. This triggered a memory of someone else's horse I knew of, it also had been driven demented by having to scratch her heels with anything she could find, so badly she had actually injured herself. She too has had this course of injections and it had made a huge difference, although I think it is something that then has to be repeated at various intervals, but I am not sure. I hoped this information gave Lucy some hope. She said that she had been concerned in case it had been related to her feeding, but he assured us that is was 'coming through the air', so was nothing to do with her management. He then pointed out that there were a lot of cows in the area, and sure enough, a few fields away there were loads of cows!

I took the opportunity to cast my eyes over his body, which I start at the front and work my way back. He immediately lifted his lip, and said, "Look, I have six teeth!" I laughed and told Lucy but said there were really twelve in front, but with a quick repeated picture, like us smiling you could only see his top teeth, so six was right! As I went down over his ears and looked at his neck, he said, "Bit of a mess, isn't it?" Oh, I felt for him. Lucy explained she had been forced to cut off his mane in a bid to help him, and quick as a flash he said, "It's okay, you could call me Tufty!"

Apart from his constant itching, he was very happy in himself and really enjoying his life with them. As I mentioned he was a family horse and was ridden by everyone, including the family dog!! Yep, he goes on board for the ride with her mum! I thought it would be lovely to ask him what he thought of the dog, Bertie, and if you were going to get a sweet reply, no, in typical Thor style, this is what we got: a picture of a small light coloured terrier panting like they do, with his very pink gums, complete with tongue hanging out, coupled with, "He looks bloody ridiculous like that!!" We both roared with laughter and I suppose to a big hairy pony looking down on this small dog puffing in front of his nose, we could maybe see his point! He did bring to our attention however that he never stands on the dog, so we realised that he could watch his feet when really needed!

On the subject of care, I knew from past experience of him, he could be rather pushy. Lucy said that he still was, especially when food was involved and asked if I could see if we could try and ask him to be gentler. I didn't even get to try, I distinctly heard the words, "I am what I am!" Some things are not up for debate and clearly he thought that was one of them! I did however 'have a bash' at the food barging as Lucy said she found it sometimes rather intimidating. I asked him what he could suggest, if he didn't mind. He showed me carrot and apples and how he could search and find them (this was distinctly confirmed by a quick tale about his bout of colic when he escaped into the orchard and landed up with a gassy belly from fermenting apples!) so could Lucy throw some into his stable for him to find? This idea was to try and break the tense time whilst he was waiting for that bucket to be brought in. She said that would be fine, and she would let me know how it went. At the end of the call, I asked him what was the last thing he would like to say, and it was, "You like a challenge, well I am a big hairy one!!"

Lucy quickly repeated that back to her husband as she thought that was more for his benefit, and he replied, "And he would be right!"

A few weeks later Lucy phoned me to book in Thor for his dental work. This had to fit in with the vet coming to sedate him, who incidentally was the same vet that had given him his next injection of 'cattle stuff' since we last spoke. Good news! The vet could see a marked improvement in his skin and demeanour so let's hope that he continues to improve. As for the 'apple distraction', it worked… for a whole two days! Thor got wise; he quickly would find them, and then dash back to the front of the stable ready to assert his authority! We did try, but typically, it was Thor who was having the last laugh!!

[1] cattle

Peppered and Assaulted!

As nearly all my work is word of mouth it is nice to be able to get a good result for someone's friend. A lady who featured in my first book with her dog, Honey, had recommended me to a lady with a tortoiseshell cat called Pepper.

This eight year old cat had her owner, Verlie, at her wit's end. The problem was a serious one, and one that is notoriously difficult to sort out, but as with every case, I can only try my best. Through her photo I tuned in to her and, to me, she seemed like your average cat with no apparent issues, until we pushed for the truth! She was weeing all over the house and apart from the smell it was making the constant cleaning was getting intolerable. I asked her to talk about it and, with some reluctance I add, she then passed the blame elsewhere. No, she was not saying that another was guilty of the weeing, she had been clearly seen so there was no doubt, but she claimed that she was in this predicament because of her brother. She went on to show me the picture of her frantically looking for a place 'to go' and gave me that feeling like you can hold on no more.

I explained this 'searching' picture to Verlie and she said, "Yes, she does go round and round and then just does it, but why not just go in her tray?" I explained that little by little we were getting the story but please do not hold up much faith in us changing this, as I was now aware she had been doing this all of her life! Suddenly she showed me a picture of a cat jumping downwards complete with a resounding thump effect to go with it. She showed me her reaction, which was, basically, to 'scram' as fast as she could out of the way.

"Verlie, do you have any idea what this is about?"

"Ah, I have been witness to this a couple of times."

"So what is happening?" I asked. Verlie explained that she had occasionally seen Dusty, Pepper's brother, jump down on top of her when she was using the tray. "What, so he jumps onto her?" I asked.

"No, onto the roof of the box the litter tray is in"

"Ah, hence the resounding thud! Oh, poor Pepper, no wonder she is frightened to go in there!" So, now we had the picture, Dusty, the naughty toad, was getting up on the work surface and waiting for the opportune moment to launch his aerial assault!

Now we had the reason, how were we going to solve it, or at least try to? I had a think and suggested that I would do my bit and that Verlie could do hers. "How can I help?" she asked.

"Well, you can 'have a word' with Dusty, and I can have a word with Pepper."

"But how is he going to understand me, that is what *you* do." I quickly told her, as I do so many people, that the only difference between her and me is that I can hear what they say back! We devised a plan and Verlie was to tell Dusty to think how he would feel if a big cat was to suddenly jump on him whilst he was going about his 'business' and, as funny as he might think how clever it is, it certainly is NOT! I told Pepper that Dusty was going to be thoroughly reprimanded and that she could bear witness to the whole thing as Verlie was going to keep a close eye on him to stop him sneaking up onto the work surface for the next few weeks.

As you may be aware, animals are very 'open' and often bark at things we can't see. This was one such case, as apart from being frightened to pee, Pepper was aware of a 'presence' in the house that was upsetting her also. The presence was just floating through from time to time and was doing no harm, so I explained to her not to be afraid and that sometimes spirits just like to come and visit where they used to live and such like. Verlie said that she would reassure her should she see her reacting to any 'odd activity'.

Within a month I had an email from one very happy owner, saying that Pepper had 'gone' in the wrong place just once more, and had not done it since. She thanked me immensely and then admitted that she had seriously considered having her put to sleep as it was making life very intolerable for everyone in the house.

This is now two years later and I contacted Verlie about this story and she informed me that all is calm in the house. Pepper was so much more relaxed, using her tray happily and as for her brother, he gave up the naughty assault game long ago.

"If you go along with your eyes shut – you don't see the bad, but you don't see the good either!"
A dog giving a great statement to try and encourage her owner to venture out into the world and actually see what good is out there also.

"It is just my body, not my spirit."
Clear words from a horse needing to go to Heaven about the irrelevance of whether her body should be buried or cremated.

"And do you know the worst thing? I can't even have babies!"
This was from a gelding that could no longer work, so couldn't offer the same services as a mare.

"I am an elderly gentleman, and elderly gentleman lounge!
A sixteen year old cat telling us what he got up to during the day.

Changing Times

When doing a communication I always make sure I establish ownership if the animal is 'elsewhere' and that all parties concerned are happy about me doing this. Although this is a story about two horses, the common denominator is a lady called Veronica.

The first booking I had was from an owner, Sue, asking for my help with her mare that was on loan to the above mentioned Veronica. The mare's name was Charley, she was chestnut, rather fine, and had a flaxen mane and tail. Sue assured me that she had full consent from Veronica for me to chat with Charley as they were having problems, and had even thought of sending her back home to Sue. I found out this pony's age, how long she had been with Veronica, and that she was actually for Veronica's daughter, Beth, to ride.

On a beautiful sunny afternoon, I sat in my conservatory and tuned in with Charley. She didn't come across feminine in any shape or form, and due to her name. I did a quick check that I had not got it wrong and this was actually a gelding we were talking to. But no, she was a mare and, although was happy to chat, came across rather like a pushy child. She would be the type that always manages to get to the front of the queue yet nobody says a word in case they cause an upset. The more I chatted, the more impatient this pony seemed to get, and Sue said, "That was her in a nutshell."

So I said, "I think this is where the problems lie. She is showing me Veronica and Beth are being ever so careful and gentle, and this is actually causing great frustration on Charley's behalf." This rang true as apparently she had started barging and been unwilling to stand still to pick her feet out, and had generally become ill-mannered. Beth was beginning to lose her confidence, as although Charley assured us that she was not actually a very fast pony (true again) but was getting bored. She wanted to go out do more, so had started to 'shy' at things just to reduce her own boredom factor!

This 'wanting to go out and do more' presented us with the other main problem. Sue asked me to ask Charley how she felt about travelling in the trailer. I was quickly shown a rather disconcerting picture of a trailer rocking and Charley made my heartbeat speed up somewhat! She was not being naughty but she would not stand still as she was extremely fearful. It turned out that about six months previously she had fallen through a rotten floor of a trailer whilst travelling along. It doesn't take much imagination to realise the horror she must have felt seeing the moving road appear under her feet. Fortunately the driver realised very quickly that something was wrong, and pulled up as soon as they could. Miraculously she was not injured, just very shaken. This, nowadays, should be a rarity and, hopefully one day will be totally avoidable as the trailer manufacturers have become aware that wooden boards will rot over time, so now they are built with a strong aluminium floor.

I had my work cut out here; she was wanting to go places so she could do more and reduce the boredom factor. Also we had to try to convince her it would be safe to travel and somehow find a way to help with the impatience problem. I levelled with Sue and said I thought the problem was due to Veronica and Beth, as they were being so careful that it was taking 'forever and a day' to get her in from the field, groomed, tacked up then ridden out. Sue agreed, as kind as they were, they were very over cautious and so we decided to let Charley help us out on this one. Fortunately, Charley was happy living with them but just wanted everything to be brought up to speed, so to speak. She suggested that, in her view, if they could get her in and ready to be ridden all within half an hour that would do just fine. That sounded fair to us, and then she made us laugh by suggesting, "You could put it to them as Charley's challenge!"

Okay, so one problem down, one to go. I explained to her that having had one accident that this actually made people doubly aware, so ensuring it could never happen again. Anyway, Veronica's trailer was the new type with a solid metal floor so it would be impossible I asked for a bonding key and Charley asked them to tell her, 'This is so we can go and have fun'. I thanked Charley for talking to me and asked Sue to pass all the information on and let me know what happens.

Roughly three months later, I got a call from Veronica herself. She told me how much my communication had helped them with Charley and now could I talk to their other pony. Just to complicate matters, he was not at their home, but was away being schooled. I said this was a bit of a difficult situation because, "If I tell you what he says and wants or feels needs to be changed, how are you going to manage to convey this to the people training him?"

"Oh, it's alright," Veronica assured me, "you know her, you have talked to her horse too!" (If you have read my first book, the lady in question was from the story about the horse that had been 'concertinaed' between two horses). I relaxed and said that was okay then and could she send me his details. They duly arrived and here was a stunning picture of Dai, a dappled grey Welsh Cob and rising five years old.

I gave Veronica a call, and this chap was absolutely delightful to talk to. They had had him since yearling and was very much part of the family. Now this is where the 'rub' came - as adorable as Dai was, he was a strong, forward going pony with a mind of his own. In fact, he did admit to sometimes 'losing the plot' but was quick to place the blame elsewhere, with the line, "I think I am too closely bred you know!" With this bit of enlightening information, I asked Veronica if she knew his breeding and could this be possible? She asked me to 'hold the line' and she would go and look at his papers. I waited with bated breath to hear the result, although by this time I have got used to horses giving me 'gems' of information you would never even have thought they would know about.

Breathless, Veronica came back to the phone, "Oh my goodness!" she declared, "His Grandfather is the same on both sides!!"

"Ah," I replied, "that definitely would explain some of his quirkiness which, basically, seems to be out of his and your control." I said that this in-breeding being a fact and, bearing in mind, from the previous chat with Charley, I knew that Veronica's daughter Beth was not the bravest of riders. So having listened to this, would it be fair to say that Dai didn't really seem suited to her?

Veronica agreed and said that she herself could not even ride him and, with that the words, "I want to jump, I want to jump, I would be able to jump big you know!" were shouted to me by Dai. I was aware that they had hoped he would be their family pony, but I simply told her what he had said. She was amazed as that was exactly what the lady schooling him had said she thought about him too! Being the unselfish owner Veronica was, she asked me to tell him that if that is what he wanted, then the trainer would start to teach him and they would go from there. The chat ended and I said that some things are meant to be, so please let me know what happens.

Before Veronica could give me an update, the lady schooling Dai contacted me about one of her new horses so I took the opportunity to ask how he was doing. She said, "Brilliantly!" Apparently, he had taken to jumping like a duck to water, was exceedingly fast, and brave with it. He had then been sold to a teenage lad who had been out winning on him that summer! I was very pleased for Dai and asked that to be passed on to Veronica. Remarkably, Charley's owner had bought a new horse and wanted me to talk to it, so gave me the opportunity to see how 'Charley's challenge' had gone too. It had gone like clockwork, (ha, ha, sorry, couldn't resist that one) but actually it did the trick: they speeded up, Charley lost most of her impatience and, best of all, travelled without turning a hair!

Beside Himself

I have to vote one of the most adorable sights is of fat, squashy, puppies lolloping around, and tumbling over their siblings. That first introduction to solid food for a litter of rapidly growing puppies is such a sticky mess filled with glee and innocence and a joyous sight to behold. This is how most puppies' lives begin and Henry, Ian's new dog, was no exception and by a stroke of good fortune, one of Henry's litter mates was living close by. He had been purchased at the same time by one of Ian's friends so life would be filled with many visits with more rough and tumble, and pulling of those oh-so-forgiving stretched lips!

Ian had bought this podgy, Black Labrador pup to be the family pet, as they had recently shunned the city lights for a healthier lifestyle and had plenty of land for Henry to run around... As a typical Lab, Henry represented his breed beautifully with complete tolerance of children and a very loving nature. He was actually a well-bred gun dog and eventually that would become another role in his life.

Time flew past, their children were growing and so had Henry, now pretty up-to-size and over a year old, it was decided to send him away for his gun dog training. Ian, his owner, consulted the breeder who recommended a trainer and, although far away in the Cotswolds, he had achieved much success on the competition field. The breeder said he would organise it all and if Henry was dropped off at his kennels he would get him transported to the trainer along with some others.

What an exciting time for Ian and Henry because in three months time he would be able to start 'working' Henry and introducing him to the social life that surrounds shooting. There is much running about and pure obedience too, as they are required to sit very still on the nearside of their handler who is shooting. For the likes of Retrievers, Spaniels and Labs, the hide-and-seek game they have to learn. They have to retrieve birds with a gentle and sensitive mouth, and bring them back to their master. For the dogs they really enjoy this as it is fun, but a honed skill. Their instinctive fascination with water is well exercised, as birds will fall far away and sometimes in ponds, so swimming becomes an obligatory pleasure.

With training complete, Ian was informed that Henry was back from the Cotswolds, so he could come and collect him. To say Henry was so pleased to see Ian was an understatement; he was absolutely overjoyed to be back! Back home he seemed rather different, and a bit quiet, but Ian thought maybe that was normal for a dog who had gone through intensive training. That Sunday, Ian phoned his friends and suggested a country walk with the two families and dogs. They met up as planned, and he opened the car door for Henry, and much to their horror, he proceeded at pace snarling at his old playmate. This quickly turned into a physical assault, to which a stop was put to very quickly, with no physical damage done. The walk didn't take place and Ian was most perturbed, but reasoned it was probably all a misunderstanding and they would be fine the next time.

Sadly, this was not the case, as when Ian was invited for a friendly day at the local shoot. Thinking it would be a perfect opportunity for Henry to have a gentle introduction, all hell let loose. Apparently Henry repeatedly aimed for every Black Labrador there, and with obvious malice. Bizarrely it was noticed that he didn't react the same to the Spaniels or Retrievers!

Ian knew someone who had contacted me regarding their dog, so thought he would ask if I could fathom out what had happened. We went through the usual booking procedure and a photo of this lovely dog arrived.

I tuned in with Henry and got an immediate sense of sadness and grief. I passed this on and Ian admitted that since he had come back from training he really was not his usual bouncy self. I delved further and then was presented with the most awful picture. I explained that what I could hear and see was dreadful and did he want to know? (I was bearing in mind that Henry's breeder had recommended this man, so I did not want to cause an upset). Ian said to tell him, and said he would use his discretion as all he wanted to do was help his dog. The vision I had been given was of a pack of Black Labradors and then this poor dog being literally thrown amongst them, accompanied by the words, "Go on, don't be so gutless!" Although the ferocity that evolved was short-lived, this would be an obvious defence reaction by a group of dogs when another is hurled into their midst. This, sadly, was repeated until this lovely, soft dog learned to 'stand his ground' and, basically, 'get in first'. Ian was appalled and saddened by such brutality but it did explain why Henry just singled out black dogs to attack.

My job was to try to undo the hurt and see what we could change, if anything. Henry was very confused and innocently asking what had he done to deserve this? I quickly dispelled this by explaining that, like a child, Ian had chosen what he thought was a nice school for him and, had he known he was being bullied, would have taken him away from it. This sat well with Henry and when Ian asked for his forgiveness, he said there was nothing to forgive. As much as I tried to convince Henry that the black dogs were not going to attack him, it was to no avail. His fear and defensive mechanisms were so strong that he just would not listen. We covered some other things and finished the call pretty much aware that his shooting career had finished before it ever started but, hopefully, with a more relaxed dog.

Ian contacted me shortly afterwards and said that Henry, in regards to normal family life, was back to his usual bouncy, loving self. Alas, the shooting career was definitely over and, sadly, so was his friendship with his litter playmate.

It must have been six months later, when I got an anxious phone call. Apparently, Ian and his wife had invited friends over for dinner and Henry acted most peculiarly towards one of the guests, Nick. Henry kept running up and barking at him in a very frantic way. For the first time ever, they actually had to banish Henry to the study until the guests had left. Could I please ask him what was it all about as Ian was very embarrassed, as was his friend, Nick, who did everything to try and be friendly to Henry but the nearer he went to him, the worse he got!

I got Henry's file back out and tuned in with him. I didn't go directly to the point; I asked him how life was and let him have his say. He told us that life was much better and he was so glad that we had reassured him that he would not be going back to the trainer. He showed me a beautiful picture of their young daughter cuddling him round his neck and said how special it made him feel.

I had to move on to the dinner party fiasco as he was not bringing it to the table, so to speak. I asked him to show me what had happened and he gave me the most bizarre vision – of a left arm, from the elbow down. Well, that totally threw me, so I asked for a repeat and the same picture appeared. I was quite embarrassed to pass the information on as it sounded so strange but I plucked up the courage and said what I could see. Mmm, silence at the other end, then Ian said he had no idea what I was talking about either. We hit onto the logics. "Did Nick, in your opinion Ian, possibly put his arm out in a way that could have seemed aggressive?"

"Definitely not," Ian assured me. In fact, he had met Henry on several occasions before, and there had been no problem.

"Did Nick's jacket maybe have some strange smell?" but in the end, I admitted defeat and said I was as confused as he was.

Ian was a true gent and said it was not a problem but thanked me for trying and mentioned that his friends would probably get in touch with me about their own dog. A thought flickered and I asked, "Err, is it by chance a Black Labrador?"

"No," was his quick reply, "it is a little Westie; sadly, his Black Lab died a couple of weeks ago," – and then I got it, loud and clear! Who had come to dinner with his master, following below his left arm? The exact type of dog, although in spirit, Henry was truly afraid of! Ian said that made perfect sense. Gosh, we would never have worked that out! I then tried to turn the negative into a positive by explaining to Henry that Nick's Lab had loved him so much, he still wanted to please him by 'staying at his heel', as that was exactly the relationship he now had with Ian too.. Henry seemed to take that on board and, again I wished them all the best.

I was working away somewhere and a text came up on my mobile saying, "You would never believe this - I am at a school rugby match and Henry has just gone up and licked Nick's left hand!"

That was just so lovely to hear, and although we could not solve all Henry's problems, the strangest one we actually had managed to get to the bottom of.

Ex'Zak'ly

In January 2010, I had a really nice feature done about me in our local newspaper by a journalist who visited me after my *Animal Insight* book had been published. We had a lovely meeting, preceded by their photographer who took some lovely photos of Sally, and somehow, managed to make me look fairly presentable as well. The article talked about the book, my work with the various outcomes and that I had even been talking to celebrities' pets too. I have been so fortunate as my book has landed up in the hands of some lovely people that many of us would recognise from TV and it is amazing who actually knows who!

Following the newspaper article, I received various emails and phone calls, which has happened before when other papers have highlighted my work. I do appreciate the efforts some journalists go to with their much welcomed enthusiasm it really does help spread the word. One Saturday morning, I took a call from Doris, who lived not that far away and was very excited to get me to do for a reading for her dog, Zak, and also buy a copy of my book. I explained to her how I worked, that once I had the photo I would give her an appointment and do it 'live' on the phone. She asked how much she was to send for the reading and book and said could I please give her my address. No problem, I rattled it off and that was that, or so I thought. Within the hour, Rolf, my wonderful guide, told me to phone her back and invite her to my house. Now that might not sound strange to you, but I generally do not ask people to my house, unless they are through a friend. Personally I wouldn't really want a complete stranger coming into our home for a reading, also it would increase the need for that horrible thing they call housework! As I work 'at a distance', there is no need, and to be honest, sometimes it can take up so much time. Without doubt, when anyone visits you start chatting about other things, but this doesn't tend to happen during a phone call. So, I picked up the phone and said, "Doris, I know you were going to post the stuff, but would you actually like to come in person to see me?"

"Yes, love," she replied and we set the time and date, which was to fit in with her work at the school and her husband, Bob's work shifts.

On a bitter January afternoon Doris arrived, chauffeured by Bob, as she doesn't drive, complete with a big smile and her photograph of Zak. I warmed to her the minute she arrived. I am guessing she has seen her fiftieth birthday, or even her sixtieth but whatever, she was petite, warm and just totally huggable. She sat herself down on my settee with husband, Bob, right beside her.

She handed me a photo of Zak, which to me sounds like a big dog's name, but this Zak certainly wasn't. He looked the cutest little fluffy Chihuahua you ever would see and I immediately started to smile. He was nearly two years old and just filled me with warmth and happiness and such laughter.

After I introduced myself, he sweetly announced, "Hello it's me!" I said that he came across as outgoing and I thought he must be rather cheeky as he showed me him tugging on one end of what looked like a towel, and taking off with it!

Doris laughed and said, "That's only the half of it," and before I could stop her, she started to tell me that he has wrecked so many things, and with that he showed me a pile of shoes!

"Mmm," I said, "were shoes on the list by chance? I am being shown a pile of them!"

"Oh yes," Doris replied with her slightly gravelly voice, and gesturing towards Bob, said, "He had yours too, didn't he?!" Bob smiled quietly and we carried on.

I asked Zak what he liked doing, and he showed me him rolling over and what looked like turning himself 'inside-out'. "Ah, there is no doubt that you are speaking to our Zak!" Doris exclaimed and, without drawing breath, she informed me, "He is very unusual, you know. Chihuahuas don't do that, they just don't - it will tell you that in the books, of which I have read many, but Zak just amazes people!" As she got 'into her stride', I had to stop her by saying that I should be trying to get this from Zak, and his opinion on things, for you - not you telling me! So, as much as you love chatting about things, I need you to let me speak.

I spotted a wry smile from Bob, who was sitting there ever so quietly, and said to him, in a tongue in cheek fashion, "I bet you will want to bring her here every afternoon!" I knew Doris would get the joke because she and I just 'hit it off' as soon as we met. Doris is one of these people that everyone adores, she works at the local school and none of the children are rude to her, they all look up to her. I think this is due to her 'down to earth' attitude, great warmth and a big heart full of giving. Communities used to be full of people like this but sadly, nowadays they seem to be a rarity.

Zak chatted away and amused us with his delightful personality, informed us that Doris is the one that tells him off (like he pays a lot of attention to it – not!), and as for Bob - Zak takes great delight in playing him up, but Bob enjoys the game just as much. Doris asked me why did Zak go and cuddle under the covers with Bob in the bedroom, but if she tries to get him to, he won't? With her, he will lie on top of the duvet, and slot himself down behind the crook of her knees instead Zak was quick to answer and said it was to do with Doris's blood pressure! I asked Doris if she suffered with her blood pressure and her face was a picture as she did. I suggested I thought it was high pressure, not low, and this was right, as Zak, bless him, said that he would feel a difference because of that, and he found it disconcerting to lie close into her chest. He was so sweet, he asked me to reassure her that it was nothing personal against her. I thought that was lovely for her to know, as lovely as it was for Zak to say.

I have to say we had had such fun. Doris had now got into the swing of this 'chatting', letting Zak have his say. He just loved the way she responded to his various quotes, (and the occasional mimicking of funny things said) with such enthusiasm and laughter, it was a joy to be part of it! When we were nearly at the 'any questions bit', Zak took great delight in announcing how clever he was, so I asked why? He said how he enjoyed the interactive toys to get him to use his brain.

"Oh, Jackie," said Doris, "now how would you know about that?"

I had to reply, "To be honest I don't really understand what he is trying to show me, but he seems to be very intent on moving something?"

"Yes," Doris said, with a certain zest of one up-man-ship I might add. "The man in the pet shop said it was for big dogs, and a Chihuahua could not possibly do it." Doris, being Doris, has sent a video to the manufacturers to admire how her little Zak, a toy breed, most certainly can do it!!

On the subject of admiring, Zak just loved being the centre of attention, and said he was, "Like a beautiful ornament," which for a showing dog, I thought very apt! This quote was to be used again fairly quickly when somehow Doris has started chatting about other dogs, and Zak promptly said, loud and clear, "You don't want a rescue!"

I repeated this to Doris, and she made me laugh with her endearing way of validating the geniality of my work, by saying, "Oh, Jackie, you are so right again! I did try to take on a rescue, which was another Chihuahua. The lady brought her round and we put them in the garden together, and she 'flew' at Zak, I picked him up and the lady picked her up and that was that, a real no go! I did feel sorry for the little dog, as she was so lovely and obviously frightened, but Zak wasn't! He doesn't care, he goes up to big and small, he loves other dogs, but sometimes they don't love him, so I am very, very careful with him." With that he then showed me a long lead and gave me a picture which led me to believe that he would run off if he was off the lead.

I said to them questioningly, "I am under the impression that if you let him off, I think he would do a runner and not come back if you called."

I got another, "Oh, Jackie," confirming that this was right, and she informed me that at training classes he did absolutely everything, but not that!! In spite of the chat about his lack of recall skills, he wanted me to put his case across as to why they did not need another dog.

This was beautifully put by him: "If I am the only ornament, then I will be polished more, therefore shine out amongst others!" I guess this would help to enhance his showing career!

Doris did have a question that was relative to showing. She had taken him to a show and he was superb in the first ring, and the judge checked him all over. Zak acted perfectly showing off his sweet personality and demeanour. Yet, in the next class, he would not let the judge near him; he cowered and hid behind Doris, refusing to let the judge touch him! I established from Doris that the judges were two separate people, and so thought I would ask Zak what was the difference from one judge to the next. He showed me the first as a fairly young person and the other, who he was wary of, seemed to be of an older generation and rather 'statuesque', which I thought was an apt description. Doris's eyes widened and she declared that I had got it right, but what was it about this older judge that worried him? Zak took me straight back to his very early days (believe you me, they can remember, and are aware of things from that early) and he showed me a lady of the same 'statuesque' build, picking up and putting down, of him and his litter mates. She was not mean in any way, but let's say, large hands with not the most gentle of scrutiny techniques was noted. Most people would not be aware of how sensitive everything feels to little ones that have had such little 'hands-on' contact, and to be turned over, have their jaw alignment checked could come as quite an uncomfortable experience. I did my best to explain to him that is was nothing personal, and that the judges just wanted to check him over, and nothing untoward would happen.

I asked him if he had any words for Doris to say to 'prompt' his memory about this conversation, and he asked to be told to, "Stand like an ornament, she only wants to check you, nothing else."

We finished our chat and I thoroughly enjoyed meeting Doris and her husband Bob. At the beginning I mentioned that Rolf had told me to invite her to come personally to my house. What Rolf knew, but I obviously didn't, was that, out of all the people that could have read the story, Doris knew a certain celebrity very well and was sure she would love to hear about me.

A couple of weeks later I took up her offer to meet Zak himself. He was wary of me at first (they apparently are suspicious little dogs), but he soon warmed to me and we had a lovely playtime. He even got to demonstrate his skill with his interactive toy - it was a set of stacked dishes, complete with sliding lids that are attached to a centre stem. So, with his nose and feet, Zak spun them round to line the dishes up properly which then made the lids pop open and let him have the treat, very clever indeed! I had a couple of hours in their wonderful company and Zak even kissed me when I left. I really have not had much to do with 'toy breeds', but if this is what they are like, I can see why people just simply adore them.

I know that Doris has told Zak that his story is being printed for all to read, and knowing that Doris is well loved in her community I am so pleased for her to be a part of this too.

In the Bank

Although lots of people come to me because they simply want to hear what their animal wants to say, the majority are looking for solutions. Celia Baker, the manager of the *Riding for the Disabled* centre at Holme Lacey, featured in my last book about a pony called Toffee. It was a very interesting case and although we found out the problem, the result wasn't exactly what she would have hoped for. Although a horse may seem suited to their job there, in Celia's mind the welfare and happiness is paramount for the horses in her care.

The next 'patient' was called Murphy, a really good stamp of a horse who had been with the RDA for just over a year. He was dark bay with a white blaze, well built but athletic with it. He had been working well and doing all that they asked, which consisted mostly of being led round with the disabled children on board. Celia having run the centre for twenty plus years knew the signs when a horse had become bored and Murphy's time had come. Some horses are in the RDA for a huge part of their life and it suits them well, but some start to 'switch off' and, again, that varies from animal to animal.

Celia thought long and hard and decided to send him back to the dealer's yard he was brought from as they would surely find him a good home again. It was a sad day for the centre as Murphy was a genuine and easy horse and would always be remembered fondly. That, basically, should have been the end of the story but no, things were really not going to plan. So once again, Celia decided to phone me and see if I, 'The Witch' (which coming from most people I would find rather unacceptable but it is her term of affection for me), could have a talk to him and find out what on earth was wrong?

As usual, Celia needed help very quickly so I didn't go down the photo route; I just got his description and age. Murphy was at this point still at the dealers yard but I was assured by Celia that she could pass on the information as she knew the dealer very well, and she was approachable. (I know dealers have a bad name and, to be honest, sadly, the majority deserve it but there are also some very good ones too. So just ask around and the ones with the good reputation will do their best to keep it that way.)

Murphy started off telling me how lovely he was but he really didn't want to go back. "Go back where?" I enquired.

"To my previous home," he answered. Now I was totally confused. He was presently unhappy at the dealer's yard but he had certainly not been at Celia's so this didn't make sense. I asked him to be clearer and it transpired we were talking about the previous home who had originally sold him to this dealer. Celia knew his background and said that he had been a hunting horse, but didn't realise there had been a problem as such. Murphy explained that he didn't want to hunt again, as he had taught a beginner to hunt and it was not the most comfortable of tasks! They had been kind to him but sometimes novice riders don't learn many riding skills before the hunting field, so can turn into a lot of 'mouth pulling' and uncomfortable 'back thudding' when landing over jumps. This would make sense to us why an animal would rather not want to repeat the process. More importantly though, he was keen to point out that he had been good enough and patient enough to put up with all this. Upsettingly, though, was that when his owner had achieved 'adequate' riding skills they had then sold him for a more up-market version! So, in his mind he felt totally let down, rather like someone practicing a starring role for a film and when it came to a public viewing being replaced by someone more glamorous! Celia knew that is why he had been 'traded in' and said she could understand that so I asked Murphy to show me how he was behaving presently.

Watching the pictures he was giving me, you would have never believed this horse had been surrounded by disabled children less than a week ago; as he was now barging and throwing his weight around; so in the end, the dealer had phoned Celia and said, "What on earth has happened to Murphy? He is not the same horse we sold you a year ago!" Obviously, Celia was dismayed and said they had had no problems like that and then got the full story from her.

Although Murphy had been good to ride and even done some jumping with them, on the ground he was like an obnoxious teenager. A lady from a large BHS (British Horse Society) equestrian centre had been to see him. This BHS Centre was for students sitting their exams and she wanted to buy a capable horse for them to ride. When she rode him he was good, not as good as he could have been but passable nevertheless, but his manners were appalling.

Unperturbed, she thought with work he would probably settle down and decided the next step was to arrange to have him vetted. The vet went out a few days later and every time he tried to listen to Murphy's heart, or try to physically examine him, Murphy would be so stroppy that he was really starting to undo his sale. The owner wanted him to have a blood test done for this vetting but, as much as this vet tried, he could not get near enough to his neck to get a vein for the blood. This was so out-of-character for him, the vets at the RDA could do anything with him. The vetting was stopped; the potential buyer was disappointed so she withdrew her interest.

Murphy showed me clearly what he had done, but, bizarrely, he was not talking to me in a stroppy way. Celia said that she understood that if he didn't want to go back to his old home that was fair enough. The problem was, if he didn't sort himself out he might have to go to the horse market and then where would he land up? I passed this all on and explained that actually he had just missed the opportunity of a fabulous home, so what did he want to do? His words, "I just want to have fun!"

"Absolutely," we agreed, "Don't we all? I replied. "This is why Celia has been kind enough to let you go, as she knew you were getting so bored." I then said, "So, Murphy, if we could find you a good home full of fun and interest, would you settle down and behave yourself?"

"Well, yes, but...," he replied, "I really would like to go back to the RDA and Celia could sell me from there!" Celia readily agreed and said the situation was embarrassing enough already. Also maybe there would be a chance she would contact the lady that was interested in him, if he agreed, to think about his actions. I put this to him, I thought it was a fair deal and he agreed and I asked for a bonding key to remind him of this conversation. He offered, "It's so you can have fun!" This was his choice so Celia could say that should any nice person come to try him.

I wished her all the best and hoped that he would keep his word. At the end of the day, he was a smashing horse and was un-enamoured with his present 'job', so, he could actually get what he really wanted.

Within a few weeks I was to meet up with Celia and several friends from our local horse community for a very sad occasion. I and so many others were lucky enough to be able to call Di our friend. Diane Lee was such an experienced horsewomen, she had a great 'eye' for the 'right' horse and just took everything in her stride. She had taught such a diversity of people, but to talk to her you would never have guessed she had actually even worked for royalty! She did, on a few occasions, mention 'The Captain' but, typically of her, it was said in such an unassuming way, I didn't even twig who she meant until someone else happened to tell me! And how funny this is - I only found out whilst writing this story that when the RDA was opened in June 1991 by Princess Anne, Di was her assistant in attendance! She was honest, caring and had knowledge and patience in abundance, both for horses and her friends alike. Sadly, in 2009 she had succumbed to breast cancer after a very long and courageous battle. She had fought the same battle ten years earlier but this time, sadly she was to lose. A couple of years ago when I found out I could do this work, Di was included amongst the people who I gave free talks to their animals. I was so pleased that I had the opportunity to share an animal talk with her. Di had been so supportive when I was fighting my own cancer battle, and although she knew she was losing hers, we had some long chats and agreed that we sure that there was more to life than just life just down here.

It was on this Friday at the church, packed with so many friends and colleagues of Di's, that I met up with Celia. It was one of those services where, although a desperately sad occasion, there were funny little anecdotes that made us all remember and smile. Someone even gave out pale blue badges with 'I knew Di Lee' on them, so fitting and the type of funny thing Di would have thought of to organise for someone else. With the service over, we set off to the local pub, as you do. Whilst walking I happened to ask Celia how the Murphy case had panned out, and she laughed and said, "Cross your fingers, he is on a week's trial, and it is up on Monday!"

"Wow!" I said, "How did you manage that?" Celia explained that she did indeed manage to persuade the same lady to come and see him back at the RDA, as he had come 'home' and become a perfect gentleman again. The lady came, tacked him up, rode him and handled him and not an ounce of barginess was to be seen.

Celia said she had forgotten how many times in her head she had repeated, "It's so you can have fun!"

Agreements were reached that they would have Murphy on a week's trial, see how he behaved and if he was good he would be vetted, and the cheque she left with Celia could be banked. Celia again said to me to cross my fingers as he had a big competition the next day (Saturday) - so here was hoping. I said I would ask my guides to help, wished her all the best and asked her to let me know the outcome.

The buyer phoned Monday evening to tell Celia she could bank the cheque with pleasure as he was an absolute star at the competition and was such a lovely sweet horse too! Celia phoned me to let me know the result, and what a result! The RDA got their money to buy another horse and, most of all, Murphy got what he wanted: Fun!

I sent this story to Celia (I always do if real identities are used) and I was delighted to hear that Murphy is adored and has turned out to be the horse that the students all love. He is so good that when given a choice the students choose him as their mount to sit their advanced exams!

This just goes to show how their thought process can be affected by memories and being able to talk to these animals really can find out why they are acting as they are. With this horse, like others before him, it just took a conversation to explain to him, just like you would a person, to put the record straight, and what a difference it make. (I am still amazed myself when animals change and I will continue trying to make it happen. It is my job to give them a voice and an ear to listen; after all we sometimes need a shoulder to cry on or someone to defend our corner for us too).

As Murphy had done his bit to teach someone on a beginner's level with all the 'unfortunates' that can go with that, how lovely that he is now appreciated for his skills at the higher level.

PENCE

Coffee with Quince

If you are thinking it is a strange combination for a title, you would be right. I have decided to let you practise your imaginary skills with this story so I am not going to help by describing the character, I will let you see what pictures your own mind conjures up.

Quince is actually the animal's proper name but on the whole he is called Quincey. As I have said, most readings come to me to help solve problems, but this one was because the owner adored Quincey and just wanted to hear what he had to say. Here is a rapidly fired collection:

"I can go sideways without looking!" was the first boast from him, and then, "There are some little 'mees' out there, you know!"

"Look, I can slide on the ice!" coupled with a lovely picture of an animal with ice-skates on, going sideways with his eyes shut!

"I don't really do much, I am just here for her to cuddle really, and that's it!"

"No, you're stupid," said to his friend.

"No, you are," the rhetorical reply.

"No, *you're* stupid!"

"No, *you* are!" a repetitive reply, from two animals squabbling just like children do, but in a comical and harmless way.

"She knew there must be something wrong with my mouth, as I wouldn't give her kisses!" he said, and then he told me, "If she says it's okay, then I trust her."

So how have your minds worked? What lovely pictures have you summoned up? What did you think? A dog/puppy? A cat/kitten? A horse/pony? Well, if you said pony, then you would have been right, but where have you seen one wearing ice-skates? Ha, just kidding! Actually, Quincey is an eleven year old Welsh Mountain pony that used to be a stallion, (before his 'operation', as he puts it) and *did* sire some 'little ones' or 'little mees', as he had said. He is grey, with huge pools for eyes and a face that says it all! He is one of the lucky ones, and has had the same owner since he was weaned from his mother.

Previously in this book, there is a story about a horse that wanted to be called Gem, well, this is actually the same owner but I could not let this story go by without telling it too. The 'stupid' banter was between Quincey and the ex-racehorse, Cash and Dash, and in spite of their huge difference in size, they spend their days happily messing about and bickering.

The kissing statement was absolutely true, and it was not as if he had stopped eating to indicate any problems. After him declaring that he was physically sound, with no problems whatsoever (true), Sheena asked me to ask him how he had got injured that stopped him kissing. Immediately I could see the impact to his jaw, but it looked more like an object, like a gate or something similar, not a hoof?! This was an accurate picture; Quincey had decided to push his head through a wooden divider to see what the filly next door was doing. She 'double-barrelled' the barrier, smashing it straight into the side of his jaw, ouch! Although not kissing, he was still eating, but needed an operation to wire it up, and for anyone that has owned a Mountain pony, you will agree it would take most more than that to stop them eating! Quincey is now famous (no surprise there) at the local veterinary practice and the 'non-kissing' story has even been repeated on talks to the public. Quincey is most delighted that people talk about him, and doubly delighted as people can now read about him too.

So, I have explained all the above, haven't I? Oh, no, the main one I have left to the end is - the reason for the title. Sheena asked me to ask if he preferred tea or coffee??!! I laughed and thought this would be a tricky one as I am not aware of many horses who drink coffee – please note, if you are now saying, 'Mine does!' you are actually talking to a book! Anyway, as soon as I posed the question I could smell coffee and said so. "Absolutely right," said Sheena.

He then showed me her cuddling him, and then said, "Oi, hurry up, I just want your coffee!!" Sheena agreed, and said that he will drink tea (and straight from the mug) but coffee he will 'mug' her for.

What a wonderful job I have, Quince was such a delight to talk to, just like a typical happy-go-lucky child. He really is the apple of Sheena's eye, so much so, that it is now a normal comment to her husband, "Okay, I am off now for 'Coffee with Quince'!"

Ah, bless!

Now, you didn't think I would let this go by without a picture did you? I had to hide them over this page as we didn't want any cheating did we?!

And just for fun, here were some of the other guesses…

JacksArt™
www.jacksart.co.uk

Postscript

I hope you enjoyed reading this book as much as I enjoyed writing it and working with the owners and animals in the cases you have now shared in. I say a big thank you to all the people that came to me with faith to try and let me help them or, simply because they wanted to hear what their animal had to say. There have been many tears shed on the way but so many moments filled with such joy, and I thank the owners who gave me their permission to write and share their wonderful animal talking tales with you.

If you have read my first Animal Communication series of books, *Animal Insight*, you may have noticed in this one I have delved slightly deeper into the spiritual side of things. With the help of my trusty guide, Rolf, I hope we have shown you that there is nothing to fear from a spiritual aspect. It is so natural, so beautiful and the most wonderful understanding that has been shown to me. When you reach the place I have, that is without fear and, living with the acceptance of, 'what is for you won't go past you', be this good or bad and see it as just simply meant to be. You can just go with the flow and enjoy the journey and make sure you make time to smell the roses on the way.

We are all here on this planet for a certain length of time, be it short or long, and that is our 'life'. I hope I have brought you some new wisdom and that you share in my reality that every day should be lived to the best possible. Always try to: help not hinder; to accomplish at least one thing, however big or small; and most importantly, share your love and bring joy to all.

Jackie Weaver
www.animaltalking.co.uk

For the cover, I have to say our Sally was the perfect model and now offers a paw as soon as anyone kneels beside her! The cat, Troodos, I had the pleasure of chatting to and as his look and name hold a special meaning with me I asked if he could be included in the picture. And finally, the Red McCaw is in honour of one that I chatted to in America who was so smart, funny and very beautiful with it.

Lightning Source UK Ltd.
Milton Keynes UK
03 December 2010

163803UK00002B/14/P

9 781907 203213